ANALYZING SOCIAL NARRATIVES

Interpreting human stories, whether those told by individuals, groups, organizations, nations, or even civilizations, opens a wide scope of research options for understanding how people construct, shape, and reshape their perceptions, identities, and beliefs. Such narrative research is a rapidly growing field in the social sciences, as well as in the societally oriented humanities, such as cultural studies. This methodologically framed book offers conceptual directions for the study of social narrative, guiding readers through the means of narrative research and raising important ethical and value-related dilemmas.

Shenhav details three classic elements of narrative—text, story, and narration—familiar concepts to those in literary studies. To the classic trilogy of terms, this book also adds multiplicity, a crucial element for applying narrative analysis to the social sciences as it rests on the understanding that social narratives seek reproduction and self-multiplicity in order to become "social" and influential. The aim of this book is to create an easy, clear, and welcoming introduction to narratology as a mode of analysis, especially designed for students of the social sciences to provide the basics of a narratological approach; and to help make research and writing in this tradition more systematic.

Shaul R. Shenhav is a senior lecturer in the Department of Political Science at the Hebrew University of Jerusalem. He is also the director of the Levi Eshkol Institute for Economic, Social and Political Research in Israel. His research interests include political narratives, political discourse, rhetoric, public diplomacy, and Israeli politics.

Routledge Series on Interpretive Methods
Edited by:
Dvora Yanow, *Wageningen University, The Netherlands*
Peregrine Schwartz-Shea, *University of Utah, US*

The *Routledge Series on Interpretive Methods* comprises a collection of slim volumes, each devoted to different issues in interpretive methodology and its associated methods. The topics covered establish the methodological grounding for interpretive approaches in ways that distinguish interpretive methods from quantitative and qualitative methods in the positivist tradition. The series as a whole engages three types of concerns: 1) *methodological issues*, looking at key concepts and processes; 2) *approaches and methods*, looking at how interpretive methodologies are manifested in different forms of research; and 3) *disciplinary and subfield areas*, demonstrating how interpretive methods figure in different fields across the social sciences.

Interpretive Research Design: Concepts and Processes
Peregrine Schwartz-Shea and Dvora Yanow

Interpreting International Politics
Cecelia Lynch

Analyzing Social Narratives
Shaul R. Shenhav

Forthcoming:

Elucidating Social Science Concepts: An Interpretivist Guide
Frederic Charles Schaffer

Relational Interviewing for Social Science Research: An Interpretive Approach
Lee Ann Fujii

Ethnography and Interpretation
Timothy Pachirat

International Advisory Board

Michael Agar
*University of Maryland,
College Park (emeritus) and
Ethknoworks LLC, Santa Fe, NM*

Mark Bevir
University of California, Berkeley

Pamela Brandwein
University of Michigan

Kevin Bruyneel
Babson College

Katherine Cramer
University of Wisconsin, Madison

Douglas C. Dow
University of Texas, Dallas

Vincent Dubois
University of Strasbourg

Raymond Duvall
University of Minnesota

Martha S. Feldman
University of California, Irvine

Lene Hansen
University of Copenhagen

Victoria Hattam
The New School

Emily Hauptmann
Western Michigan University

Markus Haverland
Erasmus University, Rotterdam

David Howarth
University of Essex

Patrick Thaddeus Jackson
American University

Timothy Kaufman-Osborn
Whitman College

Bernhard Kittel
University of Vienna

Jan Kubik
*University College London and
Rutgers University*

Beate Littig
Institute for Advanced Studies, Vienna

Joseph Lowndes
University of Oregon

Timothy W. Luke
Virginia Tech

Cecelia Lynch
University of California, Irvine

Navdeep Mathur
India Institute of Management

Julie Novkov
State University of New York at Albany

Ido Oren
University of Florida

Ellen Pader
University of Massachusetts, Amherst

Frederic C. Schaffer
University of Massachusetts, Amherst

Edward Schatz
University of Toronto

Ronald Schmidt Sr.
*California State University, Long Beach
(emeritus) and Davidson College*

James C. Scott
Yale University

Samer Shehata
University of Oklahoma

Diane Singerman
American University

Joe Soss
University of Minnesota

Camilla Stivers
Cleveland State University (emerita)

John Van Maanen
Massachusetts Institute of Technology

Lisa Wedeen
University of Chicago

Jutta Weldes
Bristol University

Shaul Shenhav's *Analyzing Social Narratives* effortlessly and expertly speaks to multiple audiences—from the uninitiated novice, intrigued by the notion of narrative but unsure what it tells us or how to study it, to the experienced narratologist. The book makes signal conceptual contributions, while providing excellent concrete guidance on how to work with narratives, and it illustrates all its points with spare but telling examples. It is sure to become a required starting point among social scientists studying the narratives that shape our lives.

—**Ronald R. Krebs**, *University of Minnesota*

Whether to found a nation, champion a political party, or rally the people in times of war, narratives serve to bind and to empassion. In this engaging and erudite book, Shaul Shenhav provides social scientists with a versatile set of tools for analyzing the social universe. In probing what it calls the "fractal logic" by which narratives multiply as they diffuse across social networks, this book exemplifies the intriguing possibilities of narrative science.

—**Raul Lejano**, *New York University, Co-Author of* The Power of Narrative in Environmental Networks

ANALYZING SOCIAL NARRATIVES

Shaul R. Shenhav

NEW YORK AND LONDON

First published 2015
by Routledge
711 Third Avenue, New York, NY 10017

and by Routledge
2 Park Square, Milton Park, Abingdon, Oxon, OX14 4RN

Routledge is an imprint of the Taylor & Francis Group, an informa business

© 2015 Taylor & Francis

The right of Shaul R. Shenhav to be identified as author of this work has been asserted by him in accordance with sections 77 and 78 of the Copyright, Designs and Patents Act 1988.

All rights reserved. No part of this book may be reprinted or reproduced or utilized in any form or by any electronic, mechanical, or other means, now known or hereafter invented, including photocopying and recording, or in any information storage or retrieval system, without permission in writing from the publishers.

Trademark notice: Product or corporate names may be trademarks or registered trademarks, and are used only for identification and explanation without intent to infringe.

Library of Congress Cataloging in Publication Data
Shenhav, Shaul R.
  Analyzing social narratives / Shaul R. Shenhav.
    pages cm. — (Routledge series on interpretive methods ; 3)
  Includes bibliographical references.
  1. Narrative inquiry (Research method)   I. Title.
  H61.295.S54 2015
  001.4'33—dc23
  2014045080

ISBN: 978-0-415-53740-7 (hbk)
ISBN: 978-0-415-53741-4 (pbk)
ISBN: 978-0-203-10908-3 (ebk)

Typeset in Bembo
by Apex CoVantage, LLC

Printed and bound in the United States of America by Publishers Graphics, LLC on sustainably sourced paper.

To Simone

CONTENTS

List of Tables and Figures   x
Series Editors' Foreword   xi
Acknowledgments   xiv

    Introduction: Being a Story-Listener   1

1   Story, Text, Narration, and Multiplicity in Social Narratives   9

2   Story: Stories and Characters in Social Narratives   20

3   Text: The Texts of Social Narratives   37

4   Narration: The Power of Narrators   47

5   Multiplicity: The Proliferation of Social Narratives   56

6   Normative Perspectives in the Study of Social Narratives   69

7   Analyzing Social Narratives   80

References   89
Index   101

TABLES AND FIGURES

Tables

1.1	Key terms in the analysis of social narratives	19
2.1	An example of a coding table for the reconstruction and analysis of stories	28
2.2	Key terms in the analysis of story	34
3.1	Key terms in the analysis of text	45
4.1	Key terms in the analysis of narration	53
5.1	Key terms in the analysis of multiplicity	66

Figures

2.1	The story reconstructed from King George's speech	35
5.1	Two Mandelbrot sets	61
5.2	From temporal dimensions to time-theme: a structural analysis of the Declaration of the Establishment of the State of Israel	63
7.1	An analytical diagram for narrative research	82
7.2	Analytical diagrams in the study of narrative multiplicity	85

SERIES EDITORS' FOREWORD

One aspect of the "interpretive turn" that has marked social science since the latter quarter of the 20th century is the turn to language, the demand to "tak[e] language seriously" (White 1992). Narrative analysis, the focus of Shaul R. Shenhav's volume in the *approaches and methods* stream of the Routledge Series on Interpretive Methods, may be seen as part of this linguistic turn. Critics, analysts, and theorists of literature have long sought to understand where the meaning of a text comes from. Initial arguments focused on the author's biography; so, if we knew that Shakespeare were gay, we might better understand the character of, say, Hamlet, according to this argument. By the middle of the 20th century, this approach was being replaced—the author is dead!—by a turn to textual aspects, such as meter, rhyme, figures of speech, and so on, which captured John Ciardi's attention in *How Does a Poem Mean?* (1959). Toward the end of the century, literary scholars were taking what might be seen as a phenomenological turn, arguing—in what is known as reader–response theory—that meaning comes from what readers bring to their readings of a text (or, in Iser's [1989] view, from a combination of all three approaches). From the perspective of "writing as method" (e.g., Richardson 1994), this engagement with readers entails "breaking through the fourth wall"—theater language referencing the imagined divide between the actors on stage and the audience. *Analyzing Social Narratives* adds other dimensions to this engagement with language, focusing on narratives created and conveyed in social settings and their interpretation at the hands of authors, narrators, audience and readers, and researchers.

What roles do narratives play in society? How do dominant and marginal narratives interact? In what ways does narrative constitute the political? How can the power of narrative in the creation of social and national identities be understood? How can dominant narratives of society, polity, and nation be challenged? The narratives we tell about ourselves—as individuals, as members of communities, nation-states, religions, workplaces, professions—are central to interpretive social and political science. Treating language in its social context, Shaul Shenhav's volume provides a succinct introduction to a methodological framework for unpacking, excavating, and understanding the impact of narratives on our lives and societies.

The study of narrative has a complex, multifaceted history, many of its analytic concepts and methods originating in the humanities, in particular in linguistics, theories of literature, and folklore studies, including the work of Vladimir Propp (1895–1970) and other theorists of a century ago. Narrative analysis is increasingly being used in the social sciences because of its power to illuminate basic social and political activities, including the building of national and other collectives' identities. It has been taken up in sociology, political science, organizational studies, humanistic psychology, nursing, planning, public policy, public administration, educational studies, and other social scientific fields. Yet these engagements with *social* narratives have imported theoretical concepts and analytic methods into the social sciences in uneven and fractured ways from humanities sources that were focused primarily on literary texts, such as poems, novels, or folktales. This has left those who want to learn about narrative analysis the choice of diving into the dense conceptual literature of the humanities, working with approaches that are not specific to social narratives, or trying to make sense of the ragtag assortment of literary theories that have filtered into the social sciences. Shenhav's book solves this dilemma by providing a solid grounding in classical narratology translated and developed for those with research interests in the social sciences.

Using an array of empirical materials, such as national anthems, declarations of independence, organizational mission statements, policy documents, and leaders' speeches, Shenhav explains each part of the classic story–text–narration triplet in a jargon-free conceptual framework. For those familiar with narratological approaches, his extension of this analytic triplet with a fourth dimension, the multiplicity of social narratives as they travel in time and space, adds a theoretical and analytic innovation. The analogy he draws with fractal geometry can aid both newer and more seasoned researchers in understanding how social narratives disperse, change, or fail to change and with what consequences for the political world. In addition to the lively examples, tables at the end of each of the four central chapters summarizing key terms plus brief demonstrations of their use, applied to the same case—a wartime speech by England's King George, make the material accessible to those new to narrative analysis. Shenhav's last two chapters round out the book, first, by providing a clear exposition of philosophically complex debates, e.g., concerning the relationship of narrative to reality, and, finally, by providing methodological guidance for thinking through the many different ways a narrative research project might be focused.

This brief book will help readers understand the power of narrative and entice them to consider how they might use this approach in their own research projects. It should help the novice narrative researcher—easily misled by the seemingly simple idea of "story" into thinking that analysis is commonsensical—to see, instead, that it requires sustained, nuanced inquiry into the many facets of narration (story telling), alongside the text itself. And it should encourage those who would dismiss narratives as "just stories" to rethink this judgment, as Shenhav demonstrates that narratives are about fundamental political processes—the building of national identity, the effectiveness of leaders, the rapid dispersal of stories, and the inexorable links between individuals' understandings of themselves in connection to their societies' past, present, and future narratives. We are pleased to welcome this volume to the series.

Dvora Yanow
Wageningen University
Peregrine Schwartz-Shea
University of Utah

References

Ciardi, John. 1959. *How Does a Poem Mean?* Boston: Houghton-Mifflin.

Iser, Wolfgang. 1989. *Prospecting: From Reader Response to Literary Anthropology*. Baltimore, MD: Johns Hopkins University Press.

Richardson, Laurel. 1994. Writing: A Method of Inquiry. In *Handbook of Qualitative Research*, edited by Norman K. Denzin and Yvonna S. Lincoln, 516–29. Thousand Oaks, CA: Sage.

White, Jay D. 1992. Taking Language Seriously: Toward a Narrative Theory of Knowledge for Administrative Research. *American Review of Public Administration* 22 (2): 75–88.

ACKNOWLEDGMENTS

While working on this book, I was fortunate to receive the help of colleagues, teachers, students, friends, and family.

First, I wish to thank Dvora Yanow and Peregrine Schwartz-Shea, the series editors. Dvora and Peregrine have been involved in the work on this book from its birth as a vague idea, through numerous versions and revisions, into this final product. I remain grateful for their profoundly useful comments and suggestions, and feel privileged working under their truly intellectual leadership.

I wish to thank my friend and colleague, Ilan Danjoux, who read the entire manuscript and offered very helpful suggestions; Yael Shapira for reviewing with me the narratological terminology and offering wonderful suggestions that helped simplify its concepts to their essence; Yael Rivka Kaplan for reading the manuscript, offering insightful comments and assisting me with technical aspects of the project; Michael Kerns, acquisitions editor, Taylor & Francis Group and his assistant, Lillian Rand, for being helpful and patient with this project.

I was also fortunate to receive help from Amit Marcus, Amit Pinchevski, Anat Schultz, David Ibgui, Doron Solomons, Gilit Ivgi, Hila Shenhav, Limor Shifman, Mor Mitrani, Nicole Hochner, Odelia Oshri, Piki Ish-Shalom, Tamir Sheafer, Yitzhak Brudni, Yohanan Plesner, and Zohar Kampf.

I am deeply indebted to Shlomith Rimmon-Kenan, Yaron Ezrahi, and Gabriel Sheffer, with whom I was fortunate to study at the Hebrew University of Jerusalem. They have been a source of inspiration and knowledge for this book.

Writing in English is always a challenge for me. I owe my gratitude to the English editors who worked with me at different stages of the project, lending their professional expertise with full devotion and goodwill: Barbara Doron, who was a great help in developing the proposal and the first draft, and Nina Luskin, who accompanied this work through endless revisions with extremely valuable comments and suggestions.

I am grateful to my family for surrounding me with the love and respect for any story, whether our own or the story of others: to my sister Dina, my brother Michael, my mother Haya, and my father Dodo (Joseph), who passed away while I was working on the book, leaving us with many good memories but also with a deep sense of loss and sadness.

I want to thank my wife, Simone, for her endless wisdom and support, and our wonderful children Miriam, Naomi, and Gad for being patient, understanding, and involved in my work mainly by constantly asking me "Daddy, did they like your book?" I am not sure who are the "they" my kids had in mind, and therefore I have never answered this question. I do hope that at least someone will like the book; if I become fortunate enough to find another one who likes the book, I can proudly tell my kids: "yes, 'they' liked the book."

Jerusalem, 2014

INTRODUCTION
Being a Story-Listener

When I meet new people I try to speak as little as possible. This is not because I am naturally a shy or passive person. I keep quiet because I want to listen—not only to what my interlocutors have to say, but also to how they say it. The way they tailor past and future, their points of views, the people they mention, the wording they use—all of these and more are cues that help me to get to know them better by listening to their stories. But it is not only individuals who have stories to tell. Our society is permeated with stories told by groups, institutions, firms, families, cities and countries, and other social actors. These stories can vary in content, form, or goals, but the benefits of listening to them remain. This book is about the value of listening to stories. Most of us can appreciate the benefits of being a powerful storyteller, but we tend to underestimate the advantages of being a powerful story-listener. This book seeks to help its readers to improve their story-listening skills by providing a systematic framework for the analysis of the variety of narratives that emerge and proliferate in the social domain, by contrast with the fictional ones that have been the focus of literary analyses.

In some respects, the analysis of social narratives is an intuitive endeavor. From a very young age we are exposed to, and produce, narratives as part of our daily communication. But as consumers of narratives, our thought processes are normally not research oriented. As a rule, people are very skillful at deriving information from even complicated narratives and are well attuned to the nuances of their tone. But our daily use of narratives does not require us to focus on the principal aspect that differentiates listening to or reading narratives from analyzing them: an attention to theoretical questions about narratives or which narratives illuminate. Instead, we let ourselves be swept away by narratives. Narratives usually "magnetize" their audiences to their agendas, making them dwell on specific events and occurrences. This, in turn, may divert attention from theoretical perspectives, the common object of academic analysis. The upshot is that, when analyzing narratives, researchers are under constant tension between the agendas of the stories and their own analytical goals.

One cannot overstate the importance of narratives in our lives. In the opening paragraph of a chapter she devotes to narrative, Ochs (1997) challenges her readers to "imagine a world without narrative," and she concludes on their behalf that this simply cannot be done: such a world is not "imaginable" (185). Indeed, a world without narratives would make things much less interesting than life as we know it: no feature films, no plots in plays or novels, no gossip about colleagues or friends. If we tried to delete narratives from our lives more systematically, we would also have to erase them from our culture and traditions: all myths, fairy tales, and superheroes would be gone; most of our sacred books would disappear; and all experiences stored in our minds as stories would be wiped away (see Ochs 1997).

To think about our world as devoid of narratives has serious implications not only for the way we understand ourselves as individuals and collectives, but also for the interrelations between those two. Narratives can connect people across generations and places (Carrithers 1991, Nelson 2003), allowing "humans to grasp a longer past and a more intricately conceived future" (Carrithers 1991: 306). Narratives can synchronize an individual's life cycle with that of a group, creating a sense of familiarity, and probably emotional attachments, even—through historical narratives—between people who live in different places and at different times, who have probably never met and never will. Giving up narratives means giving up an extremely important form of thought—one through which we interpret our personal and societal lives, express ourselves, and also store many of our personal and collective memories (e.g., Bar-Tal 2000, Bar-Tal and Salomon 2006, Hammack and Pilecki 2012, Zerubavel 1995). All things considered, it seems quite difficult to imagine a world without narratives. Perhaps that is because narratives are present "at all times, in all places, in all societies" (Barthes 1975 [1966]: 237).

Admittedly, human beings are essentially storytelling creatures (Carrithers 1991, MacIntyre 1981). Whether it is the story of our lives, of the organizations we work for, of our favorite football teams, or of our nations—we are surrounded by stories. Stories accompany people from their early childhood, and very often continue after they are gone.

People tell stories for a variety of reasons: it may be to justify themselves, to persuade, to entertain, or even to mislead (Riessman 2008). Some of these motives are quite practical. Studies using the framework of transportation theory from psychology point at important persuasive effects of narratives. It has been shown, for example, that individuals who have been "transported" into "a narrative world" become immersed in the story, "leaving the real world behind" (Green 2008, see also Green and Brock 2000). Moreover, "transportation may reduce individuals' ability to counter-argue assertions or events in the story because the reader's cognitive capacity is committed to imagining story events" (Green 2008). Such an effect reaffirms the immanent ties between narration and persuasion, which have been noted by ancient Greek philosophers, by Roman rhetoricians, and by modern students of rhetoric.

Stories help us to define who we are, who we are not, where we want to go, and where we came from. Stories contain repertoires of reactions to social situations. Accordingly, they can structure people's conceptions of society or serve as models for societal and personal behavior. In these and many other ways, stories can guide people's actions. Stories are also vital for remembering, but they are no less important for disremembering or forgetting (Norquay 1999). Forgetting, contends French philosopher and historian Ernest Renan (1990 [1882]), is a crucial factor in the creation of national and other group identities. Since storymaking presupposes selection—be it of events, characters, or points of view—what is selected overshadows what is discarded; what is told marginalizes what remains untold. In other words, whenever we tell a story, we leave out an infinite number of possible other stories, thereby committing to oblivion a myriad of characters, actions, feelings, and emotions.

Stories are also used "to mobilize others and to foster a sense of belonging" (Riessman 2008: 8). Such effects highlight the interface between the individual and the collective and show that the process of storymaking "links the individual mind to a social reality" (Hammack and Pilecki 2012: 77). This link can explain why answers to the question of why we tell stories, as well as to many other questions regarding the relations between narrative and society, are sought in interdisciplinary investigations that connect the psychology of individuals to group characteristics within a social domain.

One conceptual premise that may guide this kind of analysis is that of a "narrative identity" (e.g., Hammack and Pilecki 2012, McAdams 2001, Singer 2004, Somers and Gibson 1994). This idea pivots on the understanding that narratives can represent or shape the human experience of time. The concept of narrative identity has become a subdiscipline of personality psychology in its own right (Singer 2004: 437), and commands considerable attention in other fields in the social sciences as well (Elliott 2005, Somers 1994, Whitebrook 2001). From this psychological point of view, narrative identity can be seen as "the accumulating knowledge that emerges from reasoning about our narrative memories yield[ing] a life story schema that provides causal, temporal, and thematic coherence to an overall sense of identity" (Singer 2004: 442; see also Bluck and Habermas 2001, Ricoeur 1991). Could it be, then, that we tell stories not just because we are storytelling creatures, or because we are looking for persuasive strategies, or for the sake of entertainment? None of these reasons can be entirely ruled out, but perhaps the motivation for telling stories is much less complex and more unassuming. Simply put, through stories and their telling, we use our imagination to make a place for ourselves: a place in which we, as humans, will be able to control or at least comprehend the flow of time, a place in which we can choose the main characters and events, and sometimes also actuate beginnings and endings. These stories can be narrow in scope or epic, dry or inspiring, riveting or harrowing.

It is therefore not surprising that, on par with a political quest for control over physical territories and resources, there is an equally political quest for control over stories. Occasionally, attempts to compel an audience to identify with a certain story can be less than subtle. A telling example is George W. Bush's first inaugural speech:

> We have a place, all of us, in a long story—a story we continue, but whose end we will not see . . . It is the American story—a story of flawed and fallible people, united across the generations by grand and enduring ideals.
> *(Bush 2001)*

Bush invites his audience to step into "the American story," a long story that concatenates those who are living in a historical succession of Americans. This is a national-political story, one of many types of social stories.

But what, exactly, are social stories about? How do they differ from the fictional stories we find on our bookshelves or the ones we watch on TV? In certain respects, the answer to these questions is that there may not be much difference at all. As will be discussed in the next chapters, some elements hold for all narratives. However, other aspects of the story, as well as other narrative elements, need to be modified and adapted when social narratives are concerned. Take, for example, the truism that, in real life, social interactions need not involve any knowledge of the future. This renders problematic the notion of "closure" in social stories, which typically refer to the future. Yet, this notion is central to narrative theorizing, which by many definitions must have a beginning, a middle, and an end (this issue is discussed further in Chapter 1; see also discussion in Bazzanella 2010, Gubrium and Holstein 2009, Maynard-Moody and Musheno 2006, Shenhav 2005b: 82–3, van Hulst 2013: 631).

To the extent that no one quite knows what happens in the end, managing the expectation of closure is a critical dilemma for social actors who still wish to offer closure to their audiences. In some cases, the unknown end is a central narratological challenge faced by leaders in difficult times. For example, when British Prime Minister Winston Churchill addressed the US Congress, calling it to join forces against the enemy, he admitted that he could not foresee the future: "It is not given to us to peer into the mysteries of the future" (Churchill 1941). Gradually, however, he changed the modality of his speech from hope to certainty, admittedly in an attempt to create a semblance of closure:

> Still, I avow my hope and faith, sure and inviolate, that in the days to come the British and American peoples will for their own safety and for the good of all walk together side by side in majesty, in justice and in peace.
> *(Churchill 1941)*

The rather romantic victorious ending shows us a vivid—but also visional—picture, akin to a novel or a Hollywood film. Ingeniously, Churchill gives his audience the taste of a happy ending without specifying the character of this ending.

It appears, therefore, that stories may both guide and manipulate their audiences (Riessman 2008). While requiring active interpretation, they can nevertheless limit and constrict audience perceptions. This raises a series of perhaps the most basic and seemingly trivial, yet complicated questions in the study of social narratives: What, essentially, is a story and where does it take place? Is it on a piece of paper when written down and in the sound waves when told orally? Alternatively, is it in the minds of the audience or, conversely, in the mind of the speaker?

Take the previous example. If we agree that Churchill's words constitute a story, then where is this story? Is it in the sound waves produced back in 1941 in the halls of the US Congress? Is it in the live broadcast of the speech on the radio? Or is it in the minds of the variegated audiences who have read or heard it long after it was delivered, including the readers of this book? Moreover, to whom does this story belong? Is it owned by the speaker or by those who hear and interpret it? These questions fall together with many other key issues salient to social narratives, such as: How do narratives travel from one person to another and become social? Or even more basically, what is a social narrative? Why do we sometimes invoke the concept of story and sometimes the concept of narrative? And why do people use the terms "narrative" and "story" so differently?

This book addresses these and a range of other theoretical, methodological, and empirical questions related to the ever expanding and often challenging field of narrative research. Its writing was motivated by the understanding, shared by a growing number of students of social science, that the interpretation of narratives—whether told by individuals, groups, organizations, nations, or even civilizations—opens a wide array of options for exploring the ways in which people construct, shape, and reshape their perceptions, identities, and beliefs.

The interest that narrative insights and ideas have elicited in students of social science points to the need to adapt the basic elements of narrative analysis developed in the context of literary analysis to better serve social science disciplines. Accordingly, this book draws on the scholarly tradition of narratology, the "formal" (Ryan 2005) and "systematic" (Abbott 2008 [2002]) study of narrative—a field that emerged out of explorations into fictional writings (by scholars such as Gérard Genette, Mieke Bal, Seymour Chatman, Gerald Prince, and Shlomith Rimmon-Kenan) and folktales (e.g., Propp 1968 [1927]) and that centers "not on what narratively organized sign systems mean, but on how they mean, and more specifically on how they mean as narratives" (Herman 1999: 218).[1] Insofar as narratology offers an effective approach for understanding any kind of story in any context, its insights and ideas have permeated many scholarly fields in the humanities and social sciences, including literature, theater, folklore, conversation and discourse analysis, psychology, communication, education, history, law, and political science (for a comprehensive yet succinct review, see Czarniawska 2004; Heinen and Sommer 2009, 2010, Squire, Andrews, and Tamboukou 2013; see also Fludernik 2009: 8–12).

Occasionally, insights, concepts, and ideas of narratology have been incorporated into the social sciences directly (e.g., Borins 2012, Franzosi 2010, Jones and McBeth 2010, Patterson and Monroe 1998), but in most cases the assimilation process has been rather circuitous. As a result, a considerable number of students of social science are exposed to the concept of narrative, while lacking rudimentary knowledge of narratology. One of the objectives of this book is to correct this situation by outlining principles of classical narratology and adapting its basic concepts to the social sciences, thereby offering a framework for the analysis of social narratives.[2] It is important to emphasize that this book does not aim to cover the entire range of narrative literature and concepts, nor does it provide an overview of the history and the current state of the field of narratology. Rather, it endeavors to introduce the basic features of this discipline to students and scholars who wish to apply narrative approaches in their study of the social domain. Furthermore, one of the difficulties in narratological research is the prevalence of jargon. Thus, *The Routledge Encyclopedia of Narrative Theory* (Herman, Manfred, and Ryan 2005c) lists over 200 key terms and concepts specific to narratology, in some cases using different designators to refer to the same or very similar entity. Bypassing this dilemma, Chapters 2–5 of the present book each contains a table summarizing the concepts that appear in it, followed by a short demonstration of the analytic approach it elucidates.

As explained in Chapter 1, the treatment of narrative here adapts narratology to the societal arena by focusing on three key elements of narratives—*story*, *text*, and *narration* (Rimmon-Kenan 2002 [1983]: 3; see also Genette 1980 [1972]). In what follows, I suggest a fourth element—*multiplicity*—to capture qualities specific to social narratives. The concepts of story and narrative are often used interchangeably. As Herman (2009: 193) points out, this is mostly, but not always, the case in informal usage. The concept of story used in this book is consistent with the usage and terminology common in classical narratology, namely, as one of the elements of narrative (Rimmon-Kenan 2002 [1983]). From this perspective, "story" and "narrative" are not equivalent: while story refers to what is being told, or the "tale," narrative alludes more broadly to the act of "narrating," encompassing not only the tale but also the text and its narration. I explore this further in Chapter 1.

Chapter 2, "Story: Stories and Characters in Social Narratives," takes up the first of these three classical elements. It discusses the structure of stories and the logical links among events, plots, and story-lines; the concept of storyworld; and the roles of "characters" in social narratives, followed by a brief demonstration of an analysis of several stories. This chapter also presents the idea of master narratives and sheds light on their connection to the more traditional conceptualizations of stories and narratives.

Chapter 3, "Text: The Texts of Social Narratives," focuses on what might constitute a "text" when social narratives are concerned and where such texts can be found. This chapter points out the various kinds of narrative "texts," which may involve different modes of the communication and representation of stories, including visual images, gestures, and the architecture of spaces. These possibilities expand the traditional conceptions of texts as written or oral modes of communication.

Chapter 4, "Narration: The Power of Narrators," addresses the act or process of producing a narrative (Rimmon-Kenan 2002 [1983]: 3). It examines the element of narration at both textual and societal (i.e., extra-textual) spheres. At the textual sphere, the discussion centers on the rhetorical mechanisms of storytelling and on the different ways of telling a story to produce a range of diverse texts. At the societal sphere, the focus is on the communicative dynamic between the speaker and the audience.

Chapter 5, "Multiplicity: The Proliferation of Social Narratives," introduces the element that I wish to add to the classical triplet in order to capture a unique feature of social narratives: the mechanism of their dispersion in the social arena. This added element, multiplicity, directs a spotlight on the dynamic qualities of social narratives, analyzing them by means of an analogy with fractals.

Chapter 6, "Normative Perspectives in the Study of Social Narratives," raises and elaborates on the issues discussed in the literature on normative and ideological perspectives in the study of social narratives. These perspectives are presented for each narrative element (story, text, narration, and multiplicity). This chapter, unlike the previous ones, does not deal with the analysis of social narratives, but rather touches on some of the philosophical and normative questions surrounding it.

In the concluding Chapter 7, "Analyzing Social Narratives," the book turns to a practical approach, laying out basic guidelines for the application of narrative analysis in the social sciences. It recapitulates the four elements of narrative analysis discussed in the preceding chapters and suggests a framework for studying social narratives by applying thin and thick levels of analysis.

Using the Book

As signaled earlier, this book is intended for different audiences with diverse backgrounds and interests in the field of narrative research. It is not designed as a manual for a specific research agenda or project within the framework of narrative analysis. The book is structured in a way that allows readers to focus on chapters of interest. For instance, students of social sciences with no previous training in narrative research may be looking for an introduction to the field. Such readers may find the first four chapters most salient, especially the discussion of narratological concepts in Chapter 1. Students of literature, communication, or cultural studies with some theoretical background in narrative analysis and who are familiar with narratological concepts as presented in literary studies may benefit from the fresh perspective in which these concepts are rendered in Chapters 2–4 of this book. Scholars who are already engaged in narrative research may find a synoptic overview of what can be termed *social narratology* useful for either their research or teaching purposes. These readers might decide to skip Chapter 1, skim Chapters 2–4, and focus their reading on the idea of multiplicity in social narratives elaborated in Chapter 5, as well as on the more normative and practical discussions in Chapters 6 and 7. Or they may wish to familiarize themselves with the four narrative elements introduced in Chapter 1 and then move directly to Chapter 7, where they might find Figures 7.1 and 7.2 useful guidelines to orienting their project within the vast field of narrative research.

For example, a researcher investigating long-term mental effects of high school proms based on interviews conducted with women over the age of thirty might choose to orient the study less around the content of the stories and more on the way they are told, focusing on textual and narrational strategies. Chapters 3 and 4, which elaborate the elements of text and narration, would be the most salient in such a case, while Chapters 2 and 5, which discuss story and multiplicity, less so. In contrast, an exploration of changes that have occurred over time in a state's dominant narratives regarding its creation could be oriented toward the elements of story and multiplicity, which would suggest a careful reading of Chapters 2 and 5. If the ideological and normative meanings of dominant stories are also targeted, the section on multiplicity in Chapter 6 may likewise be deemed relevant.

Notes

1. Perhaps it is not accidental that the most important theoretical developments in narratology have been undertaken by scholars of literature and folktales, who are routinely challenged, analytically speaking, by the variety of narrative fiction produced by the human imagination.
2. Classical narratology usually refers to the work of structuralist narratologists "starting in the mid-1960s, and refined and systematized up through the early 1980s" (Herman 2009: 26). Postclassical narratology, "which should not be conflated with poststructuralist theories," contains classical narratology "but also includes more recent perspectives on the forms and functions of narratives" (Herman 2009: 26; see also the second edition of Rimmon-Kenan 2002 [1983]: 134–49).

1

STORY, TEXT, NARRATION, AND MULTIPLICITY IN SOCIAL NARRATIVES

On September 3, 1939, Britain and France declared war against Germany. The same day King George VI delivered his first wartime address—a truly remarkable speech, which is featured in the historical drama film *The King's Speech*.[1]

"In this grave hour, perhaps the most fateful in our history"—the king commenced this historic address—"I send to every household of my peoples, both at home and overseas, this message, spoken with the same depth of feeling for each one of you as if I were able to cross your threshold and speak to you myself" (George VI 1939a). From then onward the speech tells a story—that of a nation that finds itself at war for the second time in some two decades: "For the second time in the lives of most of us we are at war." The king proceeds to describe Britain's attempts to find "a peaceful way out of the differences" with the enemy. At this point the speech accomplishes something that only stories can: it evokes the experience of the past together with the possibilities for the future, all in one breath, in a continuum of events. Within it, the desirable future—"with God's help, we shall prevail"—can be told by the speaker and imagined as reality by the audience.

This and other unique qualities of narratives make it obvious why, from time immemorial, narratives have drawn the attention of philosophers, thinkers, and scholars. According to Barthes (1975 [1966]), not only does narrative "start with the very history of mankind," but "there is not, there has never been anywhere, any people without narrative; all classes, all human groups, have their stories" (237). The important role narratives play in society is at the core of Plato's concern about the potential danger stories and myths pose to his *Republic*; narrative plots constitute part of Aristotle's *Poetics*; and narratives are also discussed by Roman rhetorician Quintilian in his famous twelve-volume textbook *Institutio Oratoria*. It should not come as a surprise, then, that in his historic speech, King George decided to tell the story of Britain and its people.

This chapter lays the conceptual foundation for the book. It discusses the concept of narrative, emphasizing the importance of the story-text-narration (Rimmon-Kenan 2002 [1983]) triplet and the idea of multiplicity for the study of narratives in the social domain. The discussion also includes a definition of the concept of social narrative. In the next chapters, following a discussion of the four elements of narrative analysis, namely, story, text, narration, and multiplicity, I will return to King George's address. Apart from its undeniable rhetorical excellence, this piece can serve as a salient example for demonstrating some of the theoretical and methodological issues presented and elaborated in the subsequent chapters.

Narrative Research in the Social Sciences

According to the Global Language Monitor's Top Words of 2010, "the narrative" was the third most popular word in their global survey of the English language. It was concluded from the analysis that "'the narrative' has recently been gaining traction in the political arena" (Global Language Monitor 2010). Awareness of the uses of narrative both in academia and in daily life is on the rise among scholars in the social sciences and the humanities (Franzosi 1998, 2004).

The concept of narrative has made inroads into various fields and disciplines, stimulating what is often termed "the narrative turn" (Czarniawska 2010, Herman 2009: 23). In fact, narrative research in the social sciences is growing so rapidly (for an extensive review see Clandinin and Rosiek 2007) that, as Frank (2010) put it, "no one will ever read everything that has been written about stories and storytelling" (17).

By and large, in today's social sciences, the narrative mode is considered to be not only a basic form of communication, but also, as noted by Fischer (2003), a "mode of thought" that "furnishes communication with the particular details out of which social meaning is constructed" (179). Moreover, argues Fischer, "it is through storytelling that people access social positions in their communities, understand the goals and values of different social groups, and internalize social conventions" (Fischer 2003: 179). By virtue of their sense-making function (Fisher 1985), narratives in the social arena have a strong impact on people's perceptions of social reality both as individuals and as groups (e.g., Patterson and Monroe 1998, Shanahan, Jones, and McBeth 2011). Polletta et al. (2011), for example, claim that "stories told by groups, communities, and nations [have] created bonds of belonging and identity" (112–13); Hajer (1995) sees narratives as "discursive cement" that keeps a discourse-coalition together (65); and Carr asserts that a community "exists by virtue of a story which is articulated and accepted, which typically concerns the group's origins and its destiny, and which interprets what is happening now in the light of these two temporal poles" (Carr 1986: 128).

Fischer (2003) regards narrative as a "cognitive scheme" that imposes "coherent interpretation on the whirl of events and actions that surrounds us" (163).

Narratives, he asserts, place "social phenomena in the larger patterns that attribute social and political meaning to them" (179). As mentioned in the Introduction, this quality of the narrative form resides in the concept of narrative identity, developed by Ricoeur (1991) (see also Hammack and Pilecki 2012, McAdams 2001, Singer 2004, Somers and Gibson 1994). Narrative, according to this notion, "provides the practical means" by which persons "can understand themselves as living through time, [as] a human subject with a past, present, and future, made whole by the coherence of the narrative plot with a beginning, middle, and end" (Elliott 2005: 125). In a similar vein, Polkinghorne (1988) sees narrative as "the primary scheme by means of which human beings give meaning to their experience of temporality and personal actions" (Polkinghorne 1988: 11, see also Czarniawska 2004, Zilber 2009).

Narratives in the social domain can situate contemporary events in a broad temporal context of social experiences and involve the individual in a story of collective agency, invoking such emotionally loaded constructs as "our military unit," "the nation," or "our state." Thus, narratives enfold present social events in a time frame that extends beyond their temporal boundaries, giving the audience a sense of continuity and familiarity with episodes and occurrences that they personally could never have experienced (Shenhav 2009). From the researcher's position "[n]arratives can be indicative not only of the experiences that people have, but also of the means of interpreting those experiences that are available to them in a given culture" (Patterson and Monroe 1998: 330).

Strategies to Define the Concept of Narrative

The trajectory traversed by the notion of narrative is typical for an academic concept that gains a foothold in various disciplines (e.g., Franzosi 2010, Hyvärinen 2006) and is then appropriated in nonacademic arenas, such as the media, advertising, speechwriting, and medicine. Over the years, the interest in narratives has led to the development of many methodological approaches, anchored in different definitions and resulting in widely diverging understandings of the field's key concepts (Bamberg 2006). Scholars of various disciplines have used the concept of narrative to mean different things, making the study of narrative rather confusing. Even the widely—and routinely—used expression "narrative approach" may have become rather vague: does the term "narrative" designate the object of investigation, or does it encompass the methodological or epistemological assumptions we bring to our investigations? While the latter undoubtedly have an important part in narrative analysis, I frame my preliminary definition of narrative by identifying the features that qualify a discourse as narrative.

Perhaps the most intriguing aspect of the definition of this concept is that, while narratives themselves can be overwhelmingly complicated and rich, the actual definition of narrative can—and, in my opinion, should—be fairly technical, simple, and straightforward. Accordingly, I begin my exposition by appealing to a long tradition of scholars who defined a narrative as, first and foremost, a "thing"—an object or an artifact. However, opinions regarding the sufficient conditions for narrativity diverge based on methodological, analytical and, to some extent, normative considerations. In defining narrative, researchers in various disciplines differ not only as to the actual denotation of the term, but also in the strategies they employ. Later, I mention a number of such approaches, with a focus on a minimalist definitional strategy, which in my opinion is preferable, at least for the social sciences (Shenhav 2005b, see also discussion in Rimmon-Kenan 2006).

Let us go back to the question of what makes a certain "thing" a narrative, and conversely, why other "things" are not narratives. While one can find references to narratives as "any spoken or written presentation" (Polkinghorne 1988: 13, note however that Polkinghorne himself does not use this definition), a good starting point for defining narrative is by pointing out a premise shared, in one way or another, by most definitions—namely, that a narrative is essentially a representation of a course of events. Why is the course of events so important? Probably because this is the way we, as human beings, conceive of time. The representation of temporality, then, is a feature that makes it possible, even at this early point of analysis, to differentiate narratives from other forms of expression or thought. For example, laws, regulations, most poems, charts, and equations usually do not represent a course of events arranged in a time line, and therefore do not qualify as narratives.

Taking a minimalist strategy for defining narrative taps what narratives are, but not what they do or what we want them to do. Minimalist definitions are based on the work of narratologists from different backgrounds, who articulated the basic characteristics of narratives. For example, literary theorist Gérard Genette appeals to the conception of narrative as essentially "[a] succession of events, real or fictitious" (Genette 1980 [1972]: 25, Rimmon-Kenan 2002 [1983]).[2] Similarly, in their introduction to the book *Discourse Analysis*, Jaworski and Coupland conceive of narratives as "discursive accounts of factual or fictitious events which take, or have taken or will take place at a particular time . . ." (Jaworski and Coupland 1999: 29–30). Linguist William Labov also asserts that it is a temporal sequence that distinguishes narrative from other forms of discourse. He defines a minimalist narrative "as a sequence of two clauses which are temporally ordered: that is, a change in their order will result in a change in the temporal sequence of the original semantic interpretation" (Labov 1972: 360). It is important to note that the inclusion of additional elements in the definition of narrative limits the scope of what one considers a narrative. My considerations in using a minimalist definition of narrative are substantive in nature, namely, to avoid adding elements to a basic structural definition, as will be explained in what follows. In fact, in delimiting a set of texts that qualify as narrative according to this approach, I am being a maximalist.

While the minimalist strategy of defining narrative highlights the idea of sequence or succession of events (Abbott 2008 [2002], Franzosi 2010,

Rimmon-Kenan 2002 [1983]), some scholars adduce additional ordering criteria, as reviewed next.

Causality. A common additional criterion to define narrative is causality. History philosopher Louis Mink, for example, claims that a narrative "presumably in all cases contains a chronicle but adds to it other forms of ordering, for example causal relations" (Mink 1987: 199, see also discussion by Yevseyev 2005). A famous illustration of the presence of causality in narratives is given by novelist and critic E. M. Forster. Forster does not see causality as a necessary criterion for the definition of story but, rather, for differentiating between story and plot (see further discussion on the concept of plot in Chapter 2). He illustrates this point with the following well-known example: "The king died and then the queen died" is a story, while "The king died and then the queen died of grief" is a plot—the difference being that the second states explicitly why the queen died (Forster 1927: 130).

While it is obvious that causality can be an important element in narrative analysis (e.g., Stone 1989 and see later discussion), it is problematic as a criterion for defining social narratives. Indeed, establishing a causal relation between events is often a bone of contention in social or political debates. Arguably, social, and especially political, discourse is one of the mechanisms through which actors reach a collective agreement on causality. It would therefore be difficult, if not altogether impossible, to discuss the validity of causalities in a narrative while also regarding causality as a necessary condition to determine whether or not a given text can be regarded as a narrative. Moreover, it seems methodologically, theoretically and even morally questionable to disqualify a wide range of social texts as narratives on the premise that they do not lend themselves to causal interpretations and, by inference, to rule out the voice of their narrators. In sum, adding a causality criterion to the definition of social narrative may be counterproductive because this would exclude from the investigation material and issues that are of interest to social science scholars.

Coherence. A similar problem arises if one expects all narratives to be coherent in one way or another. On par with causality, applying this criterion would disqualify all narrators who designate successions of events but whose narratives fail to appear coherent—among them children, people in trauma, people in a state of confusion, or simply dreamers. What if someone intentionally decides to tell a noncoherent story? And what if the scholarly understanding of coherence—and, for that matter, also causality—differs from that of the speakers or their audiences?

Meaningfulness. A quest for meaningfulness of the narrative (Elliott 2005, see also Herman and Vervaeck 2005) is bound to lead us to a similar impasse. The unity of a narrative can be seen as a possible criterion for a narrative to be considered as meaningful. This criterion, which has been applied in various ways, dictates an organizing principle underlying the sequencing of events in a narrative. For example, according to Mink, in addition to causal relations, a "narrative must have a unity of its own; this is what is acknowledged in saying that it must have a beginning, middle, and an end . . ." (Mink 1987: 197, see also Steinmetz 1992). In a similar vein, White (1980) stipulates a need for causal and structural organization, that is, a "beginning, middle, and end," and consequently dismisses historical "annals" as a narrative form, on the grounds that they lack the "order of meaning" and "narrative closure" (White 1980). He likewise claims that the historical chronicle "often seems to wish to tell a story, aspires to narrativity, but typically fails to achieve it," and describes chronicles as "unfinished stories" that fail to achieve narrative closure (White 1980: 9). This demand for a structural ideal requiring beginning, middle, and end as a criterion for narrativity is rooted in the human aspiration for coherence, which narrative is expected to fulfill (White 1980: 27), and it echoes Aristotle's discussions on the nature of plot in tragedy (Aristotle 2000: Chapters 7 and 23:12, 32). However, as already argued, scholars should be aware of the obstacles posed by narrative closure, narrative coherence, and other ideals when applied to social realities, and specifically, in defining political narrative.

As discussed above, the first problem stemming from such demands is that many social interactions occur without the knowledge of what the future will bring, leaving narrators unable or unwilling to furnish endings or closures. The demand for a beginning, middle, and end gives rise to an intractable question of what constitutes an "end" in the societal arena. As soon as we expect social narratives to end with temporal or emotional "closure," or resolution, rather than with the last event in a sequence, we impose a convention concerning how to *tell* stories on the *definition* of narrative.

Leaving an issue open-ended to promote strategic uncertainty exemplifies an instance where narrators deliberately avoid using narratives with closure. Offering several future scenarios and blurring references to the future are examples of open-ended narratives that allow freedom of action—or maneuvering, as the case may be.

Structure. Some of the additional criteria for defining narrative are influenced by Labov's (1972) (see also Labov and Waletzky 1967) classical studies on what he terms "the overall structure of narratives." For Labov (1972) a fully formed narrative in casual speech encompasses the following components: abstract (i.e., clauses summarizing the whole story), orientation (i.e., orienting the listeners in respect to elements such as place and time), complicating action, evaluation (i.e., revealing the narrator's attitude towards the narrative), result or resolution, and coda (i.e., a "functional device for returning the verbal perspective to the present moment") (Labov and Waletzky 1967: 39, Labov 1972). Some who build on his work define narratives in terms of the presence of components of this overall structure, deviating from Labov's own definition of a minimalist narrative. For example, in their analysis of casual conversation, Eggins and Slade include in their definition of narrative the element of "complicating action," maintaining that narratives are "stories which are concerned with protagonists who face and resolve problematic experiences" (Eggins and Slade 1997: 239). Their definition, then, restricts the category of narrative to event sequences that are part of the complication-resolution pattern.

Effects. Other elements that have been incorporated in the definition of narrative relate to the effect of narratives. For instance, according to Toolan, "narrative depends on the addressee seeing it as a narrative . . ." (Toolan 2001: 7). In a similar vein, Coste (1989) describes the effect of being exposed to narratives as an integral part of their definition, asserting that "an act of communication is narrative *whenever and only when* imparting a transitive view of the world is the effect of the message produced" (4, emphasis added). He proceeds to point out that "[a] message is narrative not because of the way in which it is conveyed . . . but because it has narrative meaning" (5). As in the case of other elements discussed here, the question arises whether an addressee, be it in academia or in the social arena, can be legitimately designated as an arbiter who decides whether or not a message has "narrative meaning."

A minimalist definition within an inclusive approach to conceptualizing of narrative. In her discussion of the nature of the story, Rimmon-Kenan (2002 [1983]) contends that, while causality and closure may be the most interesting features of stories, "temporal succession is sufficient as a minimal requirement for a group of events to form a story" (18–19). She further notes that if we "posit causality and closure . . . as obligatory criteria, many groups of events which we intuitively recognize as stories would have to be excluded from this category" (19). In a similar vein I suggest that, as regards the social sciences, imposing more than the minimal criterion on the definition of narrative would be problematic because it unnecessarily narrows the range of texts available for analysis.

A minimalist definition, as Rimmon-Kenan pertinently points out, would also prevent scholars from singling out what may appear as inconsistent and otherwise odd narratives. In my view, such narratives should not be excluded from analysis, first and foremost, because perception of things as odd is highly sensitive to norms, culture, and fashion. Second, narratives that are inconsistent, noncoherent, or lacking closure may, in fact, be of special interest. Studying the discourse of people or groups in the wake of traumatic events, which can give rise to inconsistent narratives (e.g., Koren-Karie, Oppenheim, and Getzler-Yosef 2008, (Waitzkin and Magana 1997) or "the underproduction of narratives" due to renewal of pain and anxiety (Jovchelovitch and Bauer 2000: 68), is one example. Another would be a political tale that represents a group of people. Should a scholar be entitled to deny narrative status on the basis of what she or he sees as inconsistency, when, structurally, it includes the basic narrative parameters?

The variety of definitions proposed for the concept of narrative raises not only the question as to which of these definitions should be deemed necessary or optimal, but more fundamentally, what criteria should guide us in choosing our definition. Because defining the concept of narrative delimits the scope of narrative studies, these criteria govern the understanding of the field. In my view, in the sphere of the social sciences, one should avoid imposing aesthetic or cultural conventions on the definition of narrative. The main point is to keep the definition open, so that conventional assumptions regarding narrative do not arbitrarily exclude certain social groups from the discussion.

Metaphorically, the minimalist definition proposed here can be described as a key that enables us to enter and explore the castle of narratives. As soon as one has that key, one has full access to all of the castle's nooks and crannies—and there are no limits to the variety of styles, genres, themes, and structures that it may contain. It makes sense, then, to adopt a minimalist definition, which designates, in rather technical terms, the basic features of a narrative. Because such a definition precludes the designation of certain types of narratives as "proper," it reduces the danger of researcher bias in favor of specific genres or aesthetic conventions. This is especially important in social research, where scholars might ignore some stories only because they do not comply with their preconceptions of how a "proper" narrative should look.

The Narrative Triplet: Towards a Comprehensive View of the Concept of Narrative

So far, I have defined narrative as involving at minimum a succession of events. A more comprehensive understanding of narrative in light of its basic or fundamental components has been developed by narratologists and other scholars of literary theories. Following the French literary theorist Gérard Genette (1980 [1972]), Shlomith Rimmon-Kenan proposes an entire system of concepts encompassing various aspects of narrative. She identifies three components, found in both fictional and nonfictional narratives. One is the *story*, defined as "narrated events, abstracted from their disposition in the text and reconstructed in their chronological order, together with the participants in these events" (Rimmon-Kenan 2002 [1983]: 3, see also Lejano and Leong 2012: 3). Simply put, story is the chronological sequence of events derived from a narrative, as well as the characters involved in them. The second component is the *text*, defined as "spoken or written discourse," which undertakes the telling of the events (Rimmon-Kenan 2002 [1983]: 3). In other words, this is the mode in which the story is conveyed. The third component is *narration*, crucially, "a *communication* process in which the narrative as message is transmitted by addresser to addressee" (Rimmon-Kenan 2002 [1983]: 2). Narration, then, refers to the process of communicating the story, as there cannot be a narrative unless the story is told.[3]

These three components are in line with the understanding that narratives involve both a representation of events and the telling of those events (Carlisle 1994). This definition, as explained by Rimmon-Kenan (2006), attributes "two main characteristics to narratives: 1) events, governed by temporality, or—more precisely—a double temporality (the chronology of the events and their presentation in the text); 2) telling or narration, as an act of mediation or transmission" (10). Based on this rendering in Rimmon-Kenan's work (2002 [1983]: 2), one may suggest a more comprehensive definition of narratives, namely, *as the narration of a succession of events*.[4]

Social Narratives

The above approach to defining narrative can be applied to any kind of narrative, regardless of the circumstances or purposes of its creation. This book focuses on narratives shared, to a varying extent, by a group of people—as opposed to literary or artistic narratives, or anecdotal accounts of individuals' experiences. Conceptually, this focus can be expressed through different terminology. For instance, the term "cultural stories" refers to narratives shared and retold by all members of a cultural group (e.g., Nelson 2003: 126); "collective narratives" (e.g., Devine-Wright 2003, Salomon and Biton 2006) can be used interchangeably with "group narratives" (e.g., Saleebey 1994: 355) and seems to be the more popular term. While these concepts are not wrong in any way, in this book, I use the term "social narratives" (Durham 1998, Steinmetz 1992) for two main reasons.

First, it resonates with the basic premise of the social sciences that society "is not the sum of individuals but a distinctive entity that transcends the individual members" (Calhoun 2002: 454). This understanding of society is at odds with the concept of collective, at least in some of its uses in the social sciences. Specifically, rational choice theory often treats "collectives" as aggregations of individual-level actions (see discussion in Schwartz-Shea 2002). Possibly, this is why universities have faculties of "social science" rather than "collective science."

The concept of social narrative is more consistent with the theoretical assumptions regarding the role of narrative in human society discussed in the beginning of this chapter, as well as with the thesis, advanced in Chapter 5, that narratives in the social domain are not merely aggregations of stories but rather the product of the *multiplicity* dynamic, namely the process of repetition and variation through which narratives are being reproduced at the societal sphere. Furthermore, speaking about social narratives, rather than collective or group narratives, shows that the scholar takes into consideration both the collective and individuals.

The second reason is related to the social meanings that narratives carry. The assumption is that people narrate social meanings (Durham 1998: 195) and that the narratives we tell reflect our perceptions and understandings of society.

How, then, can we define social narratives? What qualifies or counts as a social narrative? It is possible to define social narratives as narratives that are embraced by a group and also tell, in one way or another, something about that group. Note that this definition leaves open the question about the content, the form, and the medium in which such narratives are framed. In other words, we do not stipulate what, precisely, the telling of a story about a group means. This allows us to leave open the question of what it means that a story is told "by a group." Is it told by a person who claims to speak on behalf of a group, or is it really embraced by the group or part of it? This definition leaves open other important questions, such as: Are social narratives created top-down, by social elites, or bottom-up, through individuals' stories? Or, how do social narratives change over time and with changing issues?

This inclusive definition of social narratives has significant implications for the story, the text, and the narration components of narrative, which are discussed at length in the following chapters. At this point, I mention two of these implications. The first is that social narratives involve an element of self-narration, which somewhat blurs the sharp distinction traditionally drawn between addressors (speakers or writers) and addressees (the audience or readers). I do not claim here that the notions of addressor and addressee are irrelevant—they are highly relevant, especially to the understanding of the communicational process in narration. The point is that in social narratives, speakers can sometimes present themselves and their audience as both the tellers and the hearers of a story.

The second implication has to do with the mechanisms and dynamics of the dispersion of narratives within a group of people. In order to be adopted by a group of people, social narratives must be formed through the mechanism of multiplicity, by retelling stories or, more usually, variations on stories through different means. Multiplicity ensures the circulation and integration of narratives, or elements thereof, in the societal arena. This process can be carried out orally, visually, or in writing; it can involve fiction, imagination, ancient history, shared experience, or future prospects. As long as the narrative is adopted by a group and its individual members and tells something about that group, we can consider it as social narrative.

The story-text-narration triplet opens a highly useful path in narratology for the analysis of narrative components, which are elaborated in the next three chapters, respectively. These three elements of classical narratology, which have evolved mainly from the analysis of fictional contexts (Rimmon-Kenan 2002 [1983]), are adapted in Chapters 2, 3, and 4 to the features unique to social narratives. It is important to keep in mind—especially for those new to narrative analysis—that the narrative triplet of story-text-narration is a methodological device, a means for separating and analyzing what, ontologically, is an integral whole. As discussed in Chapter 7, it is usually the intertwining of these three narrative elements that makes narrative analysis both a challenge and a rich source of insights about the human and societal condition. Chapters 5 and 7 also discuss a fourth element, multiplicity, which relates to the dynamic of narrative reproduction and is especially salient to the study of *social* narratives.

The main terms discussed in this and the following chapters are displayed in Table 1.1.

TABLE 1.1 Key terms in the analysis of social narratives

Term	Definition
Narrative	the narration of a succession of events.
Social narrative	a narrative embraced by a group that also tells, in one way or another, something about that group.
Story	the chronological sequence of events derived from a narrative, as well as the characters involved in them (developed in Chapter 2).
Text	the mode in which the story is conveyed (developed in Chapter 3).
Narration	the process of communicating the story (developed in Chapter 4).
Multiplicity	the process of repetition and variation through which narratives are being reproduced (explained and developed in Chapter 5).

Note: some of the concepts in this table are based either fully or partly on the work of other scholars. For citations please refer to these concepts in the text.

Notes

1. *The King's Speech* (Seidler, 2010). See http://www.imdb.com/title/tt1504320/ (accessed March 10, 2014).
2. Rimmon-Kenan acknowledges a theoretical possibility of single-event narratives (Rimmon-Kenan 2002 [1983]: 3; see also Blum-Kulka 1997), but notes that usually narratives consist of more than one event. However, discarding the two-event requirement is problematic, since it undermines the essential capacity of narratives to capture the flow of time in the transition from one occurrence to another.
3. The idea of the narrative triplet aligns with Herman's (2009) claim regarding the profiles of narratives. Herman asserts that "narratives can be viewed as a type of text; as a resource for communication; and as a cognitive structure or a way of making sense of experience" (7).
4. I will not focus here on Rimmon-Kenan's (2002 [1983]: 2) references to the narration of fictional events, which reflect her specific interest in narrative fiction.

2

STORY

Stories and Characters in Social Narratives

Growing up surrounded by stories, we do not always appreciate the important role they play in our personal and social lives. Stories have the capacity to portray and sustain personal experiences, desires, fears, values, and identities. By the same token, stories can be seen as central to the formation of a group and the creation of a shared identity and can also be credited with nurturing the beauty of traditions and culture. In equal measure, however, stories can be held culpable of perpetuating inequality, discrimination, racism, chauvinism, and other wrongs committed by groups. In fact, stories capture, maintain, and transfer much of human culture, or even, as some claim, are responsible for the very creation of society (e.g., Carr 1986). As such, they are "essential in the maintenance and legitimating of dominant power and ideologies" (van Dijk 1993a: 125).

So far I have discussed the concept of story as an integral part of narrative. In this chapter, I disassemble the story and identify some of its main components, such as events, plot types, and characters. The chapter is divided into two main sections. The first is an overview of the elements of story and characters in the context of social narratives, while the second zooms in on the study of stories in such narratives. Following a table summarizing the key terms mentioned or examined in the chapter, I return to King George's speech (George VI 1939a) to demonstrate the use of story and related concepts in the study of social narratives.

Stories and Characters

Stories. The term "story," as pointed out in the previous chapter, refers to the chronological sequence of events derived from a narrative, as well as the characters involved in them. Theoretically, two events chronologically related to each other constitute a necessary and sufficient condition for the existence of a story

(Rimmon-Kenan 2002 [1983]): 19). Related to the concept of story is the concept of "storyworld," which refers to "the world evoked by a narrative text" (Herman 2009: 193, Herman 2012). This notion implies that, when people are exposed to narratives, they engage in a broad range of mental processes to create the world of the narrative in their mind's eye; the idea of "storyworld" points "to the way interpreters of narrative reconstruct a sequence of states, events and actions, not just additively or incrementally but integratively" (Herman 2002: 14). In both these concepts, story and storyworld, a degree of reconstruction is necessary insofar as the story *per se* is not present *as is* in the text, but rather is inferred by the audience or researchers based on the text (see discussion in Lejano and Leong 2012).

But what constitutes an "event" in narrative analysis? A possible definition pertinent to our discussion is arrestingly simple: an event is "something that happens" (Rimmon-Kenan 2002 [1983]: 2–3). The "event" in the storyworld is conceptually similar to what it is in stories. In my view, Herman's (2009) definition of the event as "a change of state, creating a more or less salient and lasting alteration in the storyworld" (185) equally applies if the concept of storyworld is replaced with that of story. Still, the nature of an "event" merits further discussion—for instance, whether a continuing event is discrete or should be regarded as a chain of many events, a philosophical matter that is beyond the scope of this book. Nevertheless, when we see a film, watch TV, or read a book, we perceive the story as narrated events and the characters involved therein rather intuitively. For example, the tale of two jazz musicians who witness the Saint Valentine's Day massacre in Chicago, are spotted by the gangsters, run for their lives disguised as women with an all-female band, and then fall in love with the band's vocalist and ukulele player is the story of the film *Some Like It Hot*; the baby from planet Krypton having been rocketed to Planet Earth is the beginning of the story of *Superman*. The idea that, intuitively, we look at a story as a distinct element of a narrative presupposes a very basic distinction: between *what* is being told in a narrative and *how* it is told (Herman 2009: 27, see also Chatman 1978, Schmid 2010). The narrative, according to this view, includes both the "what" and the "how." The story is "what" is being told, while the text and the narration are about "how" it is told. The story of *Some Like It Hot*, for example, designates the narrated events abstracted from their disposition in the film (which also comprises motion pictures, sounds, the musical score, etc.). Note that the same events can be relayed in many different ways and through many different mediums (e.g., theater, music show, written book, and even a dance). The story will be the same or similar, but the text and the narration may be very different.

The distinction between "story"—the events themselves in chronological order—and "text"—the discourse or form in which these events are recounted—has a long tradition in the study of narratology (Fludernik 1996: 250). It was addressed in the works of Russian formalists as far back as the early decades of the twentieth century in their discussions on the distinction between *fabula* and *sjuzhet* (Herman 2009: 27). *Fabula* is coextensive with "story," in the sense this term is used here. *Sjuzhet* is taken to denote the ways in which the *fabula* is presented in the narrative text (e.g., Herman 2005a, 2005b; Lejano and Leong 2012).[1] French and American narratologists and literary critics have posited similar dichotomies, for example, *histoire* vs. *discours* or *récit* in French and *story* vs. *discourse* in English (e.g., Chatman 1978, Fludernik 1996, 2009, Herman 2009, Rimmon-Kenan 2002 [1983], Todorov 1966).

Even if one questions certain aspects of this distinction between story and text, such as the differentiation between meaning and articulation (see discussion in Rimmon-Kenan 2002 [1983]: 8; Shen 2002), from an analytical point of view it is expedient to differentiate between a story and the discourse or form in which the story is conveyed. For example, the story of the English experience of wars could and has also been told in various ways and forms, not only in King George's speech. This is especially so in regard to social narratives, in which stories become detached from a specific text and migrate from one context or medium to another (see discussion in Chapter 5).

Stories in the social domain. Many scholars of narrative analysis underscore the role of stories as a way to study either individuals or the relations between individuals and society (e.g., Nelson 2003; for a review of this shift in psychology, see Hammack and Pilecki 2012). A common method to assess single stories is through interviews (e.g., Chase 2008, Czarniawska 2010, 2004, Linde 1993. Mishler 1986, Riessman 2008). While interviews can be helpful in analyzing the social nature of stories told by individuals, social science researchers may opt to study the stories told by groups, institutions, or organizations, for example, by analyzing documents, such as declarations of independence, constitutions, and even national anthems.

Arguably, stories have a vital *a priori* role as cognitive constructs, or even as cognitive scripts, which "generate expectations about how particular sequences of events are supposed to unfold" (Herman 2005c: 514). This way of understanding the nature of stories—as preconceived cognitive patterns—has important implications for social scientists.[2] Such a perspective allows for stories that are played out in people's minds. Theoretically, then, when text and narration are missing, the element of story alone can be studied under the assumption that it is possible to analyze *what* is being told or thought out, without dwelling on *how* it is narrated.

One way to analyze stories while leaving out the elements of text and narration is by conducting polls that elicit people's stories about a specific issue by requiring them to answer open- or closed-ended questions that involve selecting certain events and characters (e.g., Sheafer, Shenhav, and Goldstein 2011, Shenhav et al. 2014). In such cases, scholars study stories that are not necessarily conveyed in a specific text, but rather encapsulate people's perceptions of stories assessed through survey questions.

In deviation from classical narratology, which traditionally has targeted mainly specific stories designated in specific texts, in social narratives, it is customary to expect to find the same story recurring in multiple different texts. Stories shared among members of organizations, firms, institutions, families, cities, nations, civilizations, or any other group of people are told and retold in constitutive documents, pamphlets issued to mark special events, "about us" sections of web pages, speeches, daily discussions, and other media. Creating ceremonial or recurring events for retelling specific or similar stories has become an important means to reinforce relations between individuals and the group. For instance, Linde's (2009) in-depth ethnographic study exploring group identity in MidWest Insurance Company points to an important role played by stories in defining both the institution and its individual members. She demonstrates how temporal events can be used, strategically, for remembering, even though this is not their primary purpose: "MidWest holds annual sales conventions in each region as well as nationally, which form regular occasions for narration" (49–50). The formal talks by the executives of the company, Linde claims, "regularly invoke the past to explain the present and the future" (50). She further notes that, in cases when new products and programs are likely to be unpopular with the agents, "it is common for management to try to show that they are actually completely in harmony with MidWest's past, which requires telling stories of this past" (50).

A favored subject in the study of stories recurring in multiple different texts is national stories. Indeed, governments go to great length to establish and sustain national stories, be it through national ceremonies, schoolbooks, or speeches by state leaders. These stories demonstrate the idea of self-narration, as they are presented as stories told by the nation to the nation about the nation (see discussion in Chapter 4). While appealing for the most part to historical events, they are very different in character from a more scientific form of historical narrative, as "stories about what a nation has been and should try to be are not attempts at accurate representation, but rather attempts to forge a moral identity" (Rorty 1998: 13).[3]

The analysis of social stories, in general, and national stories in particular, can extend far beyond the content of a specific story designated by a specific text (e.g., a single document). For instance, changes over time in the place given to historical events in national stories can tell us about important shifts in state-society relations. It is plausible, for example, that the growing attention to the history of African Americans when telling the national story of the US is indicative of the current preoccupation with human rights issues. Another direction in analyzing social stories is to evaluate similarities and dissimilarities in stories embraced by individuals, groups, or institutions. Sheafer, Shenhav, and Goldstein (2011) found, for example, that voting behavior can be explained, in part, based on similarities in the way Israeli voters tell their national story, gauged by questions in exit polls, and the way political parties tell these stories, as per their discourse in the Israeli parliament.

One of the important qualities of shared stories is their ability to carry forward information and beliefs from past generations. This may partly account for the "preeminence of the narrative form in the formulation of traditional knowledge" (Lyotard 1984: 19). The importance of stories in this regard has been recognized for centuries. For example, "telling your children" about the Israelites' liberation from Egyptian slavery is one of the 613 commandments in the Torah (the first five books of the Bible), which is fulfilled by reading the *Haggadah* book (the Hebrew term denotes an act of telling) at the Passover meal, itself an occasion for re-narrating the group's identity and its historical and textual sources.

While the role of stories in preserving and maintaining collective memories has been widely acknowledged, their important function as a tool for forgetting is no less important. As mentioned in the Introduction, the presentation of events as a story invariably involves a selection of events, characters, and points of view. Stories can thereby serve as a powerful mechanism for simultaneously discounting, silencing, and deleting an endless number of other events, characters, and points of view.

Multi-text stories, story-lines, and master narratives. A major question that often arises in narrative analysis in the social domain centers on the interrelation between the story and the text, or texts, that conveys that story. The text–story relationship affords three major analytic options.

The first is the straightforward case of *one text, one story*. For example, if someone tells the story of his or her life in an interview, the text for this story is a transcript of that interview. A single text can also be a conversation, a speech, a commercial ad on TV, or anything that counts as a textual unit based on the broad definition of text taken up in Chapters 1 and 3. In the social sciences, the assumption of a one-to-one relationship between a delimited, book-type text and the story is hardly tenable. While in many discourses, such as certain types of speeches and interviews, the connection between text and story is fairly straightforward, in numerous other cases it is by no means self-evident.

A second option is *one text, many stories*. In this case, a single text contains more than one story. Such instances occur quite frequently in narrative research. For example, interviews in which different experiences are raised, or speeches utilizing various personal cases to demonstrate an argument may incorporate more than one story. In fact, there are no clear rules for differentiating among stories in a single text, and this issue may be subject to debate in each separate case. Disagreements may arise regarding the division of the text into stories or story-lines in which events are "restricted to one set of individuals" (Rimmon-Kenan 2002 [1983]: 16). At times, what seems to some as different stories or different story-lines may appear to others as episodes or "segments" of a single story. The end of one story and the beginning of another may be signaled through a change in settings or characters, but in every case the analytic demarcation is always a matter of interpretation.

A major focus of attention and one that reflects many social scientists' interest in broad and collective perspectives are stories that are anchored in texts created by several people or institutions. Accordingly, a third option is *one story, several texts*. Some stories surpass the boundaries of a single text. For example, national stories are usually expressed in an eclectic corpus of texts found in different sources, such as school textbooks, ceremonies marking memorial and independence days, preambles to constitutions, and even national "places," such as museums, cemeteries, statues, and visiting centers of major institutions (parliaments, palaces, courts, etc.). In many instances, a scholar may identify a story relying on several texts, such as different interviews or different newspaper articles. This third option in which a single story resides in more than one text seems to be particularly characteristic of social narratives, in which stories are shared as they are told and retold by a groups of people (see Chapter 5). In such cases, scholars can regard different narrative texts featured on different occasions as parts of one bigger story. The idea of "one story, several texts" is aligned, to an extent, with the notion of master narrative and other related concepts such as metanarratives (Lyotard 1984) or grand narratives (see discussion in Bamberg 2004, 2005; Patterson and Monroe 1998: 325–6).

The notion of master narrative has been interpreted in a variety of ways. A common denominator in all these discussions appears to be that stories in the social domain reflect or evolve from leading principles, widespread ideologies, or socio-cultural perspectives, which themselves can be conceived of as master narratives (Bamberg 2004, 2005). The importance of master narratives for the analysis of social narratives stems from the understanding that narrators are themselves subject to the influence of master narratives, and therefore the texts they produce may tell the same or similar story. Note, however, that although master narratives are sometimes defined as a narrative about other narratives or as a story about other stories (e.g., Auerbach 2009: 295, van Eeten 2007: 256, see also Somers and Gibson 1994), they do not necessarily qualify as a story or narrative according to "the narration of a succession of events" criterion, discussed in Chapter 1. Whereas stories are driven by the specific nature of events and characters (Schmid 2010), master narratives are propelled by general principles.

In another approach, Deborah Tannen (2008), in a study on sisters' discourses, suggests the concept of *Big-N Narratives*, which reflect the major themes—in her case, derived from the interviews she conducted for the study. This concept is situated somewhere between *small-n narratives*, recounting specific events or interactions, and master narratives, which she sees as culture-wide ideologies shaping the Big-N Narratives.

Characters in the social domain. In narratology, a character is "a text- or media-based figure in a storyworld, usually human or human-like" (Jannidis 2012). An intuitive scholarly understanding of the role of characters in stories rests on their characterization in the text: based on the information in the story, the reader formulates a perception of the people figuring in it and their motivations. When it comes to social narratives, however, the public's understanding of the characters and occasionally also scholarly interest in them are formed somewhere in the interface between their textual characterization and their conduct outside the text. This duality, or possibly coexistence, between the text and the world outside the text is at the core of Aristotle's concept of *ethos*, which refers to the representation of the speaker or other characters through speech. All in all, in social narratives, a mutual projection invariably exists between the characters in the stories and the social actors they represent.

Characters in social stories are not necessarily individuals. Characters representing groups of people are part and parcel of social narratives. Take, for example, Thomas Jefferson's characterization of the "nation" in his first inaugural address:

> A rising nation, spread over a wide and fruitful land, traversing all the seas with the rich productions of their industry, engaged in commerce with nations who feel power and forget right, advancing rapidly to destinies beyond the reach of mortal eye.
>
> *(Jefferson 1801)*

The list of characters representing groups appears endless, including the nation, firms, institutions, organizations, political parties, the government, our world, or our planet. It comprises personal pronouns such as "we," "us," and "them," (e.g., Mitrani 2013) and also abstracted ideas or values such as "democracy," "tyranny," or "peace"—all of which can be personified.

Such understanding of characters in social narratives has two important implications. First, insofar as most characters in social narratives are "borrowed" from the real world, humans have a natural propensity to perceive characters as "real." Yet, this authenticity is not at all imperative and, in some cases, even outright impossible. In fact, it would be naïve to assume that characters in social narratives constitute a direct or objective representation of "real" actors or issues.

The second implication has to do with a narratological dilemma regarding the criteria for evaluating characters. If a character is human-like, one can impute to it human characteristics, even if only as an analytic strategy. Yet, it is not at all self-evident that such projection is possible in regard to clearly non-human characters, such as countries, institutions, or firms. As with other key issues, the approach depends on the purpose of the analysis. If a scholar seeks to understand real actors through their representation in a narrative, she or he should not rely on the personification of social actors. On the other hand, if the main goal is to understand the role of characters in the story, or the way speakers perceive or present characters, personification can serve as a useful tool. For example, when, referring to France in his farewell speech, Napoleon Bonaparte said, "I go, but you, my friends, will continue to serve France. Her happiness was my only thought" ("Je pars. Vous, mes amis, continuez de servir la France. Son bonheur était mon unique pensée") (Bonaparte 2005 [1814], Lacretelle 1829 [in French]: 187), thereby framing France as a human-like character. In studying contemporary France, it might be bizarre to see the state as a person, but it would not at all be odd to do so when studying France as represented by Napoleon.

The Study of Stories

For the purpose of research, stories can be reconstructed from a text by writing down the narrated events, as well as the characters involved in them, in chronological order. A more advanced stage of this technique will also show how these elements are related to one another. Among other purposes, this may be helpful for juxtaposing stories told in various contexts and/or through various modes. For example, in a study of Israeli school system ceremonies commemorating assassinated Israeli Prime Minister Yitzhak Rabin, Vinitzky-Seroussi (2001: 254) discusses how left or right political orientations affect the time frame of the story. Stories can also be compared based on their chronological orientations (e.g., past vs. future). For example, comparing the stories told by Israeli government ministers with stories on the same issues told in parliament allowed me to follow the construction of historical multitemporal discourse in the transition from confidential in-camera discussions to open forums (Shenhav 2005a). Studying stories can also help to trace their variations and changes, in terms of both the presence and the absence of major events, as well as relations between events.

Methodologically, reconstructing stories from a narrative makes for an easy and straightforward way to study narratives. It refers to the analytical work done by a researcher to strip or peel off textual and narrational elements from a narrative, leaving only the chain of events and characters involved in them. To identify and study the stories systematically, a researcher may opt simply to write down the events in chronological order or, more elaborately, to categorize or code the texts—for example, according to periods of time and characters—and then arrange the coded texts according to a chronology of events. This can be achieved by using a simple Excel file or table (see Table 2.1 for an example). A researcher can, for example, number the paragraphs, summarize main events, and identify actors/characters and temporal references, the latter either relative to other events (by inferring their order) or, if feasible, by marking down the actual time designated in the text (Table 2.1 assumes that a single paragraph may reference multiple time periods, and therefore, as discussed later, for each paragraph scholars can decide whether a temporal category appears or not). Table 2.1 represents the continuum of the text by the course of paragraphs. Other organizing logics can also be employed. For example, there are other ways of tracing the temporal trajectory of a text. Benoit and Sheafer's (2006) content analysis of televised debates applies Holsti's (1969) idea of theme, defined as "a single assertion about some subject." As explained by Benoit and Sheafer (2006: 286), themes can vary in length from a phrase to a paragraph. Such tables enable a comparative analysis of stories along various parameters, such as event types, typical characters, and future/past orientation.

TABLE 2.1 An example of a coding table for the reconstruction and analysis of stories

Numbered paragraph	Text	Events	T1 Pre-birth era	T2 Past experiences	T3 Future	T4 Distant future	Characters	Comments on text	Comments on coding
1	copy-paste text fragments (optional)	describe main event	yes/no	yes/no	yes/no	yes/no	list of characters	observations	issues regarding the coding of the text
2									
3									

Note: T1 . . . T4 represent predefined periods of time.

Note that, while any competent reader or listener is capable of reconstructing the story from a narrative, the outcomes of this analytical strategy are likely to vary at least to some extent. The divergences can result, for instance, from different understandings of what constitutes an event (see the discussion above), a varying degree of detail (e.g., whether the reconstructed story includes all subplots, every action and character, or just the major ones), or different interpretations regarding the relations between events (e.g., temporal, causal). All in all, the reconstruction of stories from a narrative involves scholarly judgment, in the sense that there is no mechanistic, stepwise method for reconstructing the (events that constitute the) story from the text. Yet the differences can be diminished if, in analyzing a narrative, scholars have some basic *a priori* agreement about the reconstruction of stories (e.g., regarding the degree of detail of events and characters or to what extent relational categories should be part of the story).

This kind of agreement could involve preparing, in advance, a taxonomy of stories. For instance, timelines of social stories can be charted based on predefined temporal categories. Theoretically, this categorization may be very general (e.g., past/future) or rather detailed (e.g., every year from the beginning of time to an eternal future). Institutional stories (e.g., produced by organizations, states, sport clubs, etc.) can be categorized into four general time periods: *Pre-birth era (T1)*: from the beginning of recorded time (including references to mythical ancient times) to the day when the institution was established; *Past experiences (T2)*: from the emergence of the institution until the events that took place immediately prior to the creation of the narrative text; *Future (T3)*: hypothetical or conclusive references to the future; *Distant future (T4)*: based on general references such as "the next generation" and "long term," the researcher can determine what constitutes the long-term future in any given case, as people usually tend to refrain from dating future events. Note that these four categories do not incorporate the present time, as it is often difficult to determine whether or not a narrative text refers to the present—for instance, when it comes to general observations or in descriptions of feelings and thoughts. However, if references to the present time are of interest, the researcher can set up rules to categorize it for the purposes of a specific study. To facilitate a more nuanced analysis it is possible to create more detailed tables. For example, the analyst might separate the column representing events into subcolumns referring to a predefined list of typical topics or add more options to the time line.

Studying relations between events. As shown earlier, in addition to temporality, there can be other types of relations that are all part and parcel of stories. One of these is *causality*. Although, as already argued, causality should not be part of the definition of story, this does not mean that it has no importance as a means of connecting events in a story. Indeed, the purpose of many stories in the social domain is to establish or disestablish causal connections, as those who control the story in the social domain are in a good position to control perceived causalities. This is not to say that the causalities of stories that group members perceive as compulsory are necessarily correct. It does, however, say a lot about the connections between such stories and perceptions of particular causalities as correct or true. Likewise, in many political debates, attempts are undertaken to establish different causalities by the use of "causal stories" (Stone 1989), either implicitly or explicitly. For example, discussions in the wake of terror attacks suggest a wide range of causal relations, typically attributing the attack to military or security weakness, a lack of political solutions, and the evil nature of the perpetrators. Clearly, these and other suggested causal relations that link events in various policy or political discussions are not objective; rather, they are ideologically or other value-driven "readings" of current affairs. However, the telling of a political story is not merely a reflection of one's take on reality but also a means of imposing one's version on others. It follows, therefore, that causal relations in stories about political affairs usually carry a political purpose, though it may be hard to tell whether it is the political bias that structures stories or whether stories structure the political bias. For example, it is likely that being a vegetarian will affect the way one tells the story of meat production—for instance, by adopting the point of view of an animal. It is equally likely, however, that such stories can change people's beliefs and make them vegetarians.

The evaluation of causality in social narratives can take very different paths. The most basic is to identify the causal relations between events as represented in the text. This technique targets the informative or descriptive level of the story, that is, event X leading to event Y. Alternatively or additionally, a researcher may look for causal relations within the narrative, but rather than identifying explicitly stated causalities, find them by inferring from what is said.

The following statement by US President Lyndon Johnson about the US war in Vietnam can serve as an example:

> Why are we in South Vietnam? We are there because we have a promise to keep. Since 1954 every American President has offered support to the people of South Vietnam. We have helped to build, and we have helped to defend. Thus, over many years, we have made a national pledge to help South Vietnam defend its independence.
>
> *(Johnson 1965)*

In his explanation of the US presence in Vietnam, Johnson explicitly based the causal relations between events on a commitment to a promise: in the past, the US helped South Vietnam and offered support; it is to keep its promise that the US is now "in South Vietnam." A researcher may, however, search for implicit causal relations between the events. For example, the text insinuates that there is more than a "promise" or a "pledge" behind the US presence in Vietnam. The two concluding lines of the excerpt reiterate the promise-based causality (in this case, the "pledge") but also add two important elements: the material element implied by the words "we have helped to build," and a national security element, alluded to by invoking the US help "to defend" Vietnam. These two elements can be interpreted as an additional reason for the presence of the US in Vietnam, namely, its national interest. Such inferred causal relations are invariably the product of analytic interpretation.

Another type of analysis evaluates the fidelity of causal relations in the story to those in the "real" world. Reverting to the previous example, a researcher can evaluate to what extent the presence of the US in Vietnam is, indeed, the result of a promise. While many students of social narratives opt for this approach, it is, arguably, the most difficult and sometimes even impractical for examining causality in narrative. More often than not, we have no clear grounds to judge which causalities represented in social narratives occur in the real world, and to what extent—especially when such relations become a bone of contention in social life. A telling example in the political domain comes from the 2008 economic crisis. Consider a statement taken from a speech delivered by Barack Obama—at the time a US Senator from Illinois—campaigning for the presidency. Obama opens his address by acknowledging the problem: "We meet at a moment of great uncertainty for America," and "The economic crisis we face is the worst since the Great Depression." Then he goes on to state: "We cannot allow homeowners and small towns to suffer because of the mess made by Wall Street and Washington" (Obama 2008). Here, Obama references the great depression of the 1930s by blaming "Wall Street and Washington" for the current crisis. It stands to reason that his desire to attack his opponents plays a major role in his choosing a particular cause to account for the current crisis. Although many stories pivot on causal relations, scholars should be wary of imputing this logic to social reality. However tempting the idea that stories about society capture causalities in social relations may be, causal relations in stories are not necessarily based on careful analysis of causality in social events. Rather, the way people envision causal relations between events can be affected by, or even replicate, fictional conventions or their own interests. What is more, the human tendency to impose narrative conventions, for example of drama, tragedy, or a complication-resolution structure, on social reality may induce a person to base his or her causal inferences on generic conventions that do not parallel, and may oversimplify, social relations.

An instructive method to investigate connections between events in a story is "event structure analysis" (ESA) (Corsaro and Heise 1990, Heise 1991). This approach allows for a number of options for linking between events, in addition to straightforward causality in which one event or action is the cause of another. One is establishing *prerequisite* relations, which gauges whether one event or action requires another event. A somewhat looser or softer link is *implication*, which probes whether an event implies another event. A third option is *counterfactual* relations, in which the analysis poses a "what if" question so as to probe whether removing certain events from the narrative or modifying some of the facts could alter the course of narrated events (Griffin 1993: 1103, see also Ponti 2012). Heise (2014) demonstrates the potential use of such counterfactual strategy: the researcher is to ask a question of the type, "Suppose an action like ____ does not occur. Can ____ occur anyway?" (16). Following Weber (1949 [1905]), Griffin (1993) notes that, in historical narratives, such questions—for example, how would US history have evolved if the Civil War had not been fought?—can be helpful in evaluating the significance of causal relations.

Relations between events are also affected by the nature of each one, as the distinction drawn between *kernels* and *catalysts* (sometimes *satellites*) makes evident. Kernels are events that "advance the action" in the story "by opening up new alternatives or possibilities, whereas catalysts are events that "expand, amplify, maintain or delay" previous events (Rimmon-Kenan 2002 [1983]: 16, see also Chatman 1978). The kernels/catalysts dichotomy facilitates an analysis of a course of events by focusing on the construction of continuance and changes by a story. A typical example of the role this dichotomy plays in social narratives is the way institutions and organizations frame the moment of their establishment using kernels. For instance, the story of the founding of the World Health Organization (WHO) as told in one of its brochures starts with a meeting of diplomats in 1945: "When diplomats met in San Francisco to form the United Nations in 1945, one of the things they discussed was setting up a global health organization. WHO's Constitution came into force on 7 April 1948 . . ." (WHO 2007: 4). This kernel event is followed by others that are catalysts. The latter refer to the developments that build on the 1948 occurrences: "WHO's work has since grown to also cover health problems that were not even known in 1948, including relatively new diseases such as HIV/AIDS" (WHO 2007: 4).

The study of plot and plot types. The concept of "plot" takes the researcher beyond the events and the connections between them and allows him or her to differentiate among various story types, or genres. This term, typically used to designate "the ways in which the events and characters' actions in a story are arranged" (Kukkonen 2014), keys in on the content of the story and what it is about. However the concept of plot is only vaguely demarcated and has been used in a variety of ways, for example, as a synonym for "story," as the creation of causal relations between events in a story (see discussion on causality in Chapter 1), or as a cognitive notion describing "the attempt to make sense of a larger, unorganised entity by imposing some kind of reductive and selective explicative system of order on it" (Dannenberg 2005a: 437, see also Kukkonen 2014).

The concept of "plot type" is usually more specifically defined and has to do more with "the story that a narrative tells" than with the "more complex conceptualizations of plot" (Dannenberg 2005b: 439). The question of plot type can be addressed through genre-based categories such as comedy, romance, and tragedy; through a repeated formula such as detective stories; or through narrative movement such as improvement and deterioration (Dannenberg

2005b: 439). Also relevant are structural elements, such as happy endings (see discussion of Churchill's war speech in the Introduction) or complications and their resolutions (e.g., Labov and Waletzky 1967). An example of the use of plot type in the public domain can be found in Obama's (2008) speech discussed earlier. Obama's utterance blaming "Wall Street and Washington" for the economic crisis is aligned with the prototypical plot type in contemporary American politics in which "the government in Washington" or "the people in Washington" are dubbed the "bad guys" who should be held accountable for everything that goes wrong in the United States. Like many other political speakers, Obama links together as a villainous protagonist the usual target of left-wing ideological criticism, "Wall Street," and of right-wing ideological criticism, "Washington."

From a theoretical point of view, turning a sequence of events into a plot is termed *emplotment*. This term was coined by Hegel and popularized by historian Hayden White, (Czarniawska 2004), who defined it in the framework of historiography as "the way by which a sequence of events fashioned into a story is gradually revealed to be a story of a particular kind" (White 1975: 7, see also Polkinghorne 1988: 54, Czarniawska 2004: 20–2). White further elaborates that emplotment refers to the transformation of chronicles, or sets of events, into well-established genres of plot types, such as romance, tragedy, and comedy (White 1975: 7). Later on, this idea was reformulated in broader terms as "introducing logical structure which allows making sense of the events" (Czarniawska 2010: 62). This latter understanding of the concept of emplotment renders it relevant, far beyond historiography, as an important mechanism that imbues a set of events with ideological and moral valence by appealing to preexisting plot types. In the example above, Obama explained the economic crisis by adhering to conventional political stories with conventional villains. By the same token, social actors or researchers can draw on classical plot types, such as "tragedy," to tell or to understand social narratives.

Plot types can have broad social implications, especially under the assumption that some of them can structure audience expectations regarding narratives. For example, a plot type can have ideological salience "because it might rehearse particular patterns of thinking" (Kukkonen 2014), endorsing particular ideological expectations such as social or gender roles. Moreover, in a culture where narratives for public consumption are expected to be patterned according to the complication-resolution structure, a story that deviates from this plot type is likely to be met with rejection and mistrust.

Identifying established plot types in a particular society can also help researchers to appreciate the difficulties of integrating new narratives into the social domain. Consider, for example, political leaders telling public stories with peacemaking plots in the wake of long-lasting conflicts. Complication-resolution (Labov and Waletzky 1967) is a fundamental plot type in this context, and its use to justify a peace initiative is fairly common. This strategy, however, is highly vulnerable to counterattacks and delegitimation through arguments and contending stories. In peace negotiations any story designed to bring about resolution will encounter obstacles, for various reasons, such as uncertainties about the peace process. But the complication-resolution plot type is especially likely to be resisted since, in a transition from war to peace, and especially in the wake of continuing conflicts, counterstories contending that resolution can only be based on the use of force are usually well entrenched. That is a major difficulty faced by governments engaging in negotiations with organizations that were hitherto perceived as terrorist, against which it is necessary to use military force so as to achieve "resolution." Yet, in a peacemaking story, the use of military force is part of the problem, or "complication." Peacemaking stories face yet another difficulty, which has to do with their main protagonist. This is the villainous protagonist who is strongly associated with the problem, or "complication," of the story and who is expected to be instrumental to a proposed "solution." Such stories, then, require a drastic metamorphosis in which both the "complication" and the protagonist of yesterday abruptly become part of the "resolution."

The main terms and techniques for analyzing stories in social narratives discussed in this chapter are arranged in Table 2.2.

TABLE 2.2 Key terms in the analysis of story

Term	*Definition*
Story	the chronological sequence of events derived from a narrative, as well as the characters involved in them.
Storyworld	the world evoked by a narrative text.
Master narrative	leading principles, widespread ideologies, or sociocultural perspectives from which stories in the social domain evolved.
Plot type	the kind of story that a narrative tells—can be addressed through genre-based categories, repeated formulas, narrative movements, or structural elements.
Emplotment	turning a sequence of events into a plot.
Kernels and catalysts	*kernels* are events that open up new possibilities. *Catalysts* are events that expand, amplify, maintain, or delay previous events.
Reconstructing stories	a basic technique to identify stories in a narrative by writing down the narrated events, as well as the characters involved in them, in chronological order. A more advanced stage shows how these events and characters are related to one another.

Note: some of the concepts in this table are based either fully or partly on the work of other scholars. For citations please refer to these concepts in the text.

Demonstrating the Study of Story

Let us return to the example of King George's speech to demonstrate the study of story. The story can be reconstructed from the speech and displayed graphically (see Figure 2.1). The rectangles represent the events mentioned in the speech. As is rather common in political discourse, which often operates with more than one possible future, this particular story contains several futures, which are manifested in the text in the form of (a) certain outcomes, (b) semihypothetical, realistic situations, and (c) purely hypothetical scenarios. These multiple futures are displayed in Figure 2.1.

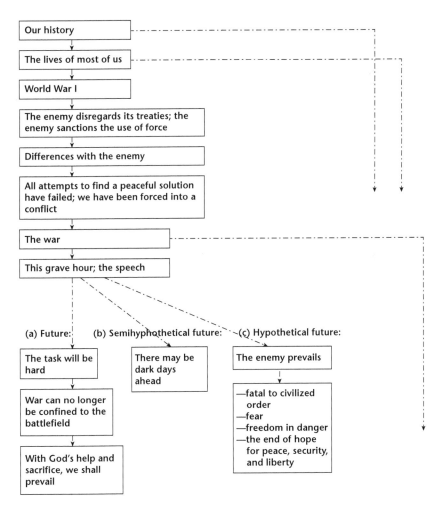

FIGURE 2.1 The story reconstructed from King George's speech (George VI 1939a)

Note: The broken arrows represent the continuation of events.

Even a cursory analysis of this story affords several thought provoking insights. The story incorporates an aggregation of personal aspects (the "lives of most of us"), international and political affairs (referred to as attempts to find a peaceful solution), and the divine perspective (God), as the intended audience of the address is an imagined community that rests upon three main pillars: the people, politics, and God. In this sense, this brief analysis reveals that the King's speech does more than tell a story about the outbreak of the war with Germany; it conveys, through a story that brings together individual and group perspectives, a sense of the national consolidation of British society on the brink of war.

Another aspect that is disclosed by reconstructing the story from that text is the structuring of the future. As argued in the Introduction, closures in social narratives can be difficult to arrive at, for the future is unknown. A common way to concretize possible future scenarios is by describing hypothetical worlds. In the speech, these "futures" are followed by a kernel anchored in the present time ("In this grave hour, perhaps the most fateful in our history"). The story is emplotted by means of a seemingly clear closure in the form of a happy ending, embodied in the assertion "We shall prevail." But when the story is reconstructed, the picture becomes far less clear. First, in addition to the "we shall prevail" scenario, an alternative hypothetical future is presented (see hypothetical future in Figure 2.1) that emphasizes the disastrous implications of losing the war, thereby legitimizing a military effort. The binary opposition between the divinely assisted future outcome, on the one hand, and a catastrophic culmination of the story, on the other, offers two possible endings—prevailing over the enemy versus losing the war. Yet, in addition to the above dichotomy, there looms a more weakly demarcated, yet clearly perceptible interim, semihypothetical option of "dark days ahead." In this perspective, the impending conflict on the battlefield is portrayed as enigmatic and unresolved. Unlike the two other "futures," it points to no concrete course of events. It is suspended in midair, as it were—possibly as an allusion to the actual state of affairs at that time, in which no one really knew what the future would bring, or as an insinuation that some dark days might lie ahead even in the case of a "happy" ending.

Notes

1. For a detailed discussion on different angles on the *fabula* vs. *sjuzhet* dichotomy, see Schmid (2010: 175–85); Lejano and Leong (2012) apply this dichotomy to hermeneutic analysis of public controversies.
2. See, for example, Ish-Shalom's (2013) concept of the "lighthouse narrative" that "shapes our expectations about the future and guides our individual and collective behavior" (82).
3. Tensions between national stories as told by states and by historians are likely to occur if only because historical research is less conservative than traditional, governmental ways of narrating.

3
TEXT
The Texts of Social Narratives

Of the three main elements of narrative—story, text, and narration—text may be the most commonsensical term, conceptually, as captured in this definition: "The wording of anything written or printed; the structure formed by the words in their order; the very words, phrases, and sentences as written" (Oxford English Dictionary Online Edition). While this is a good departure point for understanding the nature of text, it is certainly not enough.

This chapter points out the various "incarnations" of text, depending on the mode in which stories are communicated and represented. An overall discussion on the element of text in the context of social narratives is followed by practical suggestions for the study of text. The chapter concludes with a table summarizing the main terms followed by a demonstration of their use in analyzing King George's speech (George VI 1939a).

Text in Social Narratives

Where social science is concerned, the commonsensical understanding of text as a set of written words must be broadened. Even if researchers follow the convention whereby texts are things with written words, they still have to keep in mind that texts can take many forms and modes other than the usual ink-on-paper, computer, or tablet displays. Graffiti, stickers, or minutes of meetings are some other examples of social texts. We should also take into consideration the possibility of oral and visual modes of conveying stories. Visual gestures, dance, silent movies, and oral storytelling are all versions of texts. Physical places and physical spaces, such as built spaces (Yanow 1995) or memorial monuments (e.g., Young 1993, Zerubavel 1995), can also be treated as texts.[1] When talking about texts, an inclusive approach would take into account all possible ways of conveying stories. In light of this, how should text be defined? The definition suggested in Chapter 1 frames the text as the mode in which the story is conveyed. A reasonable definition should also pivot on the idea of text as a physical object, as the text is, first and foremost, concrete and physical. It can be embedded in segments of ink, pixels on a screen, sound waves, visual images, and even body language. As long as a text designates a story, we can regard it as a narrative text. This approach distinguishes text as the medium from story as the content.

The material aspects of texts (e.g., production and distribution technologies) do not as a rule preoccupy students of narrative analysis, being usually of more interest to publishers, producers, engineers, computer scientists, and experts in telecommunication. Still, the ramifications of this topic should not be disregarded by narrative research scholars (e.g., St. Clair's 2004 study on the history of books). For instance, new telecommunication technologies, social networks, and e-books affect the dispersion of narrative texts worldwide, and this has a direct bearing on the ubiquity of texts in society. However, for most of the concepts and theories discussed here, the question of format (e.g., hard copy, on screen or smart phone) is immaterial.

What is the content of narrative text? First and foremost, narrative texts convey stories. This does not mean that every section of a narrative text designates a sequence of events (see discussion in Labov 1997, see also Jovchelovitch and Bauer 2000). Descriptions, judgments, observations, and numerical data are all examples of the kinds of content that do not convey events, but which one can expect to find when studying texts that tell stories.

From a cognitive-pragmatic perspective, it is possible to see narrative text as a set of instructions for the human mind to evoke stories and characters. A story enclosed in a text can be told in a variety of ways. Salient questions in this regard include style, rhetorical devices, metaphors, similes, and numerous other techniques of composition. Yet, narrative texts are more than merely a technical means for communicating stories. Even such a basic aspect as the order of events presented in the text can be extremely important, both for the effect of storytelling and for understanding the storyteller. In telling a story, it is more common to move backward and forward on a timeline than to follow chronological order. In narratology and cinematography, these techniques are termed *flashback*, or *analepsis*, for going backward in time and *flashforward*, or *prolepsis*, for anticipating future episodes (Herman, Manfred, and Ryan 2005a, 2005b, Ireland 2005, Rimmon-Kenan (2002 [1983]).

When it comes to social narratives, the temporal relations between text and story can be especially meaningful. For example, when a text starts and ends with the final event of a story, it expresses circularity, which is absent when the same story is told in chronological order. A linear chronology from earliest to latest, in contrast, is often used to create the impression of authenticity and credibility, as it is supposed to represent the course of time. This way of organizing events in the text can be found in official reports, legal descriptions, and parliamentary reviews that ministers create and present about their ministries. While chronological narration may contribute to credibility by imitating the flow of time, it can also make a story boring, dry, and jejune. This is not necessarily a drawback, especially when the narrator prefers the story to be shelved without attracting much attention—as, for example, some ministerial reports for parliament.

Textual necessity. For most narratologists who work on literary theory, the mode in which a text is presented is rarely an issue, as the texts they work with—mostly novels—are usually concrete: written and bound. But in social narratives, much as in folktales, the nature of the text poses a greater challenge. This is especially so when dealing with such actors as a firm, a nation, a government, or, on a more abstract level, a revolution—all of which can be part of narrative texts channeled through a variety of modes and means. Ignoring the element of text may lead to an amorphous and misleading conceptual understanding of narrative, rendering this term equivalent to other concepts, such as "approach," "perception," or "ideology."

On a more general note, it is important to ask whether texts are necessary for social narratives. After all, not all stories are embedded directly in a text. Dreaming, fantasizing, or simply musing about past events—all these processes may give rise to stories devoid of texts, bolstering the case for text-free narratives. This may be so, but in order for such narratives to be converted from individual to public status, they require a text that will carry them from one person to another. This does not mean that research cannot explore stories that are dissociated from a text. For example, it is possible to learn about people's preferred stories by using surveys about stories' events and protagonists (e.g., Sheafer, Shenhav, and Goldstein 2011; Shenhav et al. 2014). While it would be problematic to term such survey results narrative "text," they can be regarded as a *post factum* documentation of stories or parts of stories. Still, to the extent that stories are *social*, they must have, at some point, been transmitted through a text, whether oral, written, or graphic. In other words, if a story is in the public domain—it has probably been told somewhere, in some form, by someone.

The Study of Texts

The study of texts opens up a wide variety of options to examine the ways of telling stories in social narratives. Descriptions of places, the tone and nuances of messages, characterizations of protagonists—these and many other aspects can be studied as part of text analysis.

The study of points of view. One of the important benefits offered by the study of text is the opportunity to analyze the points of view embedded in social narratives. *Point of view* (also known as *focalization*) is a concept stemming from the idea that stories are always mediated by a certain prism, perspective, angle of vision, or center of consciousness (Miller 2005, Rimmon-Kenan (2002 [1983]).[2] Although most of these expressions are optical metaphors, the concept itself should be understood more broadly, as encompassing a "cognitive, emotive and ideological orientation" (Rimmon-Kenan (2002 [1983]: 72).

As noted by Rimmon-Kenan (2002 [1983]: 73, see also Linde 2009: 75), the researcher should be open to the possibility that those who narrate the story are not necessarily the protagonists whose point of view is reflected in the narrative. Quite often, narrators represent several different points of view, which cannot be adequately examined through the study of story alone, but require a sensitive textual examination. Take, for example, the words of Winston Churchill, in his historic address to the US Congress in December 1941:

> I am a child of the House of Commons. I was brought up in my father's house to believe in democracy. "Trust the people." That was his message. I used to see him cheered at meetings and in the streets by crowds of workingmen way back in those aristocratic Victorian days when as Disraeli said "the world was for the few, and for the very few." Therefore I have been in full harmony all my life with the tides which have flowed on both sides of the Atlantic against privilege and monopoly and I have steered confidently towards the Gettysburg ideal of government of the people, by the people, for the people.
> *(Churchill 1941: 226)*

This quote incorporates many "voices." In addition to Churchill's personal point of view, the text cites Churchill's father, Disraeli, and Lincoln (by referring to his classic Gettysburg Address). Yet, the presentation of points of view goes beyond references or allusions to various individuals. Churchill brings in an institutional perspective through reference to a set of formal points of view—those of a British prime minister and the British nation, and to some extent, also the mutual Anglo-American perspective. In addition to these institutional, national, and bi-national angles, the text offers yet another set of points of view anchored in values. The text expresses the perspective of Churchill as a child, both literally and figuratively: as his father's child and as "a child of the House of Commons." Next follows the perspective of the father himself, as he instructs the young Churchill to "trust the people." The father-son perspective then becomes political, not only by virtue of the father's message, but also in Churchill's observation of the crowds, both in Parliament and in the street. Through the image of the crowd, and specifically, by referring to Disraeli's statement about the world in aristocratic Victorian days being "for the few, and for the very few," the text incorporates a societal perspective. It is at this juncture that Churchill's point of view as a political leader comes into view, as he ties together "both sides of the Atlantic" and makes a stand against privilege and monopoly. Through quotations, both direct and indirect, through the attribution of text to institutional and national players, through allusions, and through changes of focus, these multiple points of view are integrated into the text and are presented as normative political perspectives.

As this example amply illustrates, identifying and tracing various points of view can be helpful in evaluating the normative perspectives built into social narratives. Narrative texts that seek to represent a number of different people and groups will by definition integrate more than one point of view.

Exploring points of view in texts usually goes hand in hand with analyzing the characters present in the narrative. In the study of stories, the scholar focuses on characters' actions. Textual analysis probes deeper into the ways characters perceive the world, whether the one within or outside the story. Many questions can be raised in this connection. An analyst may, for example, probe the individual-group continuum, looking specifically at whether the narrative conveys the point of view of an individual, a group, an institution, a nation, or humankind in general. Questions can likewise be asked about the relation between the point of view and the story (e.g., Linde 2009), for example, whether the former is attributable to a character in the story or to a contextual entity, such as the person who created the narrative, an organization, or perhaps even a deity.

Time, text, and context. Text analysis is often associated with exploring the element of time in narrative. The study of time is extremely complicated, both philosophically and perceptually. From an analytical perspective, a key to understanding time in narratives may be found in the interplay between the flow of events designated in the narrative text, on the one hand, and the story that can be constructed based on these, on the other (Rimmon-Kenan 2002 [1983]: 44).

A useful distinction can be drawn between *story-time* and *text-time*. Story-time refers to the linear succession of events and derives from the story (Rimmon-Kenan 2002 [1983]: 44). Polkinghorne (1988) explains that story-time "is understood to be an objective time where events are ordered sequentially and where time units are equal" (92). The following description of Levi Strauss & Co. posted on their corporate website illustrates this concept:

> Founded in San Francisco by Bavarian immigrant Levi Strauss in 1853, we created the very first pair of jeans. Today, our products, sold under the Levi's®, Dockers®, Denizen®, and Signature by Levi Strauss & Co.™ brands, are loved and trusted by people from all walks of life.[3]

This is a simple and straightforward narrative, ostensibly based on factual information, entailing story-time that starts in 1853 and ends today.

By contrast, text-time refers to the "disposition of elements in the text" (Rimmon-Kenan 2002 [1983]: 45) or the "linear (spatial) disposition of linguistic segments in the continuum of the text" (Rimmon-Kenan 2002 [1983]: 44). It is considered linear because, when humans read or hear a text, they experience it as a one-directional process, letter after letter, word after word (Rimmon-Kenan

2002 [1983]: 45).[4] Text-time can be evaluated in spatial terms, such as by following the words, pages, or paragraphs in a text passage dedicated to portraying the events of the story, or in temporal terms, based on the duration of the reading or hearing. Defining time in narrative fiction as "the relations of chronology between story and text," Rimmon-Kenan (2002 [1983]: 44) notes that both story-time and text-time are in fact pseudotemporal, and somewhat problematic. Story-time is a conventional construct that people fashion when exposed to narrative texts, while text-time is no less spatial than temporal. Exploring the interrelations between text-time and story-time can still be a very fruitful approach to the study of narratives, as discussed in the next section. When it comes to social narratives, I believe that a third dimension should be added to the binary story-text temporal distinction, which I term *context-time*. Context-time is not the temporality represented by the story, which can contain fictional elements or be entirely fictional. Nor is it an equivalent of text-time, which is confined to the boundaries of a specific narrative. Context-time is the time in which readers or listeners live, before, during, and after they are exposed to narratives. It can be conceptualized as the ticking of a clock, as a calendar on the wall, or as flux.

The context-time dimension can serve as an important reference point in analyzing temporal processes while decoding a narrative and "interacting" with its narrators. Humans are usually aware of their own time of day and the current date. They have plans for the afternoon or for the following day. They have personal memories, as well as goals and prospects for the future. All these can be aspects of context-time. Crucially, the audience of narrative experiences the overlapping between context-time, text-time, and story-time. In persuasive narratives, the context-time dimension can be supplanted, at least partly, by the latter two as the audience is transported into the storyworld. In this transmission process, text-time plays an especially important role insofar as it constitutes an interface between context-time and story-time. That is, text-time draws the listener or the reader from his or her personal context-time into story-time.

The narrative text can, and has been, used as a cornerstone in many a social and political endeavor, notably when a leader may have sought to make his or her audience experience a transition from context-time to story-time. A compelling narrative text made it possible for Winston Churchill to transform the dark tale of fear and anxiety into a long and heroic story of stubborn endurance and resistance—freedom against tyranny. A narrative text can serve as a means for a charismatic CEO to present the nine-to-five work routine as a wonderful journey and to offer a fascinating vision of prosperity. It is the text that renders the recycling of a single plastic bottle part of a millennia-long history of the earth and humankind. The potential effect of successful social narratives is evident in what is termed "memorial discourse." Such narratives not only endow the loss of individual life with historical meaning, they may also transport the audience to a legendary world in which the dead are resurrected and rejoin the living, as part of the sublime story of nationalism.

The transition from context-time to story-time is one of the magical moments in social narratives. This is where individuals' time frames merge with those of other individuals. Note, however, that the experience of being transported by a narrative into story-time does not mean that humans necessarily lose their sense of context-time. Indeed, people can be present in context-time and story-time simultaneously, in what can be called a multiple temporality experience.

By way of illustration of the experience of multiple temporality, imagine that today is August 28, 1963. You arrive by bus in Washington, DC, to participate in the famous March for Jobs and Freedom. On your way to Washington you meet several human rights activists like yourself. It is early afternoon, and together with over 200,000 people, you stand in front of the Lincoln Memorial. You are thinking about the long day you have had and about the long way back home. You chat with the friends you met. Then Dr. Martin Luther King, Jr., takes the stage. Luckily, you had come early enough to stake out a good spot, so you can hear the words: "Five score years ago, a great American, in whose symbolic shadow we stand today, signed the Emancipation Proclamation . . ." (King 1963). At that point, guided by Dr. King's story, you feel yourself transported back a hundred years in American history. You proceed, in historical time, past the Emancipation Proclamation to the Gettysburg Address, to which King alludes in the opening part of his speech. You move forward in time as King goes on to state that "100 years later the Negro still is not free" (King 1963). You share a dream for the future that "one day this nation will rise up and live out the true meaning of its creed" (King 1963). You have experienced all that, vicariously, through his speech, even as you are still standing with your friends, in the crowd, on August 28, 1963. This is the multidimensional experience of time afforded by a narrative text. This example can be rendered even more complex if now, as the reader of this book, you again become part of the experience. You are experiencing the process described above: your context-time is spent reading these lines, while the text compels you to visualize yourself back in 1963 in Washington, DC, and takes you further back in time . . .

Order, duration, and frequency: three questions for the study of time in narratives. Following the work of Genette (1980 [1972]), Rimmon-Kenan (2002 [1983]: 46) suggests analyzing the concept of time in narratives, utilizing the relations between story-time and text-time, with respect to three concepts: *order, duration, and frequency*. Statements about *order*, she explains, "would answer the question 'when?'" in the chronological sense: first, second, last, before, and after (Rimmon-Kenan 2002 [1983]: 46, see also Herman and Vervaek 2005: 60–1; Polkinghorne 1988: 93). Statements about *duration* "would answer the question 'how long?'" in terms like an hour, a year, long, short, from x till y (Rimmon-Kenan 2002

[1983]: 46). Statements about *frequency* "would answer the question 'how often?'" (Rimmon-Kenan 2002 [1983]: 46) in terms like X times a month, a year, a page of speech, or an interview.

Traditionally, *order*, *duration*, and *frequency* are examined through the interrelationships between the text and the story. To study *order* is to analyze events designated in the text vis-à-vis their order in the story, using such concepts as flashback and flashforward (see the discussion earlier). The study of *duration* rests upon a relation between two durations: the duration of the story as it transpired and "the length of text devoted to it" (Rimmon-Kenan 2002 [1983]: 52; for a slightly different definition, see Herman 2009). Measuring duration presents a considerable challenge. One method is based on assessing the relation between the amount of text (for example, by counting words or measuring the time it takes to listen to the text) and the corresponding length of time in the story that the narrated events took to unfold. For example, it takes approximately one minute of slow speech to utter one hundred words. In these one hundred words, or one minute, it is possible to narrate a story spanning a hundred years, but it is also possible to relay a course of events that occurred in less than a minute. Notably, some stories or parts thereof are told in a more condensed manner than others (Rimmon-Kenan 2002 [1983]: 53).[5] The study of *frequency* can be undertaken by examining "the relation between the number of times an event appears in the story and the number of times it is narrated (or mentioned) in the text" (Rimmon-Kenan 2002 [1983]: 57)—which is easy to measure. In social narratives, the frequency of designated events can carry some important implications. On an intuitive level, the retelling of an event can be interpreted as underscoring its importance. However, it might be the case that speakers seek to conceal most important events. The question of frequency is also relevant for certain types of illness and post-traumatic stress disorder that have been found to be associated with narrative texts that are characterized by repetitions, discontinuities, and fragmentations (e.g., Frank 2013 [1995], Kosenko and Laboy 2013, Rimmon-Kenan 2002 [1983]). Accordingly, frequency can also allude to a state of mind following a trauma.

While *order*, *duration*, and *frequency* are traditionally examined through the interrelationships between text and story, it might be analytically expedient to relate these categories to context-time. A scholar might, for example, incorporate context-time in the study of text-time and story-time, inquiring "when?", "how long?", and "how often?" regarding the story, the text, and also the context. This premise entails that, at least to some extent, the context or the "reality" can be arranged in a narrative form—a pattern that allows its examination on the basis of order, duration, and frequency. This assumption, however, is contested, as will be elaborated in Chapter 6, as part of the discussion of the story-vs.-reality debate.

The main terms used in analyzing the element of text in social narratives are presented in Table 3.1.

Text: The Texts of Social Narratives   **45**

TABLE 3.1 Key terms in the analysis of text

Term	Definition
Text	the mode in which the story is conveyed.
Point of view	a concept stemming from the idea that a story is always mediated by a certain prism, perspective, angle of vision, or center of consciousness. It encompasses a cognitive, emotional, and ideological orientation (also known as focalization).
Story-time, text-time, and context-time	three dimensions of time in social narratives: *story-time* refers to the linear succession of events in the story; *text-time* refers to the disposition of linguistic segments in the text, which is usually conceived of as a linear sequence because the process of reading or hearing texts is unidirectional; *context-time* is time in which readers or listeners of narratives live.
Order, duration, and frequency	three concepts to study time in narrative, gauged by the questions of "when?", "how long?", and "how often?", respectively.

Note: some of the concepts in this table are based either fully or partly on the work of other scholars. For citations please refer to these concepts in the text.

Demonstrating the Study of Text

Let us return to King George's speech and reread, for now, only the first paragraph, probing the relations between the *order* of the events relayed in the story and the connection between context-time and the story-time produced by the text.

> In this grave hour, perhaps the most fateful in our history, I send to every household of my peoples, both at home and overseas, this message, spoken with the same depth of feeling for each one of you as if I were able to cross your threshold and speak to you myself.
>
> *(George VI 1939a)*

In this preamble, the king positions himself in the present but immediately refers back to "our history," thereby assuming the point of view as if he were standing at a temporal and spatial crossroad. Against this backdrop of history underscoring the significance of the present hour, the king takes a wishful spatial "journey" to "every household" in order to deliver a personal message to all his subjects. It is due to this imagined situation in which the king visits every household that the audience experiences the transition from context-time—the fateful hour that they face alone—to a historical experience that they share with the king.

It is as though the text began with a story of telling the story. Before the actual story is told—the references to the previous war (WWI), the justification for the current war, the attempts to prevent the latter, and the promise that "with God's help, we shall prevail"—its main point has already been conveyed by the act of sending a message. Considering the importance of leadership in times of conflict, the choice of such an opening for a speech marking the beginning of a war makes a lot of sense.

Studying the rest of the speech may lead the analyst to note that the text repeatedly refers to a future war, even though—or, perhaps, because—it is an event that has not yet happened. Textual examination also attunes the researcher to word choices. For instance, by describing the main principle governing the enemy's actions as "the mere primitive doctrine that might is right," the text characterizes the enemy with negative valence insofar as the word *primitive* has negative meaning and as the proverb *might is right* connotes vulgar popularity and crudeness. Another telling observation is that nowhere in the speech does King George refer directly to the enemy as "Germany"; instead, it is presented as a "principle."

This illustration exemplifies the potential contribution of incorporating textual elements into the study of story. In its turn, by focusing social narrative analysis on such aspects as word choice and points of views, as well as the order, duration, and frequency of events, the study of story enriches the researcher's perceptions and observations regarding the material at hand. Metaphorically speaking, if the story is the skeleton of a narrative, the text seems to be not only its flesh and blood but also to some extent its soul.

Notes

1. This approach aligns with Taylor's (1971) idea of "text analogue," suggesting that acts can also be treated as text (see Yanow 1995, 1996, 2014).
2. Rimmon-Kenan (2002 [1983]), therefore, prefers the concept of focalization. However, to refrain from introducing unfamiliar terminology, I will use the term "point of view," especially since this concept seems to be sufficiently broad and intuitive for the purposes of social research.
3. http://www.levistrauss.com/about (accessed November 15, 2013).
4. Cases of analogy might tone down this claim (see Rimmon-Kenan 2002 [1983]: 154, note 2).
5. For instance, while investigating the structure of political narratives, I found that many of them contain a condensed textual unit in which the text designates the entire temporal frame of the story in a few words or sentences. This issue will be elaborated and illustrated in Chapter 5. These textual segments, which I have termed *concise narratives*, are extreme cases, in that long periods of story-time are manifested in very short segments of text (Shenhav 2005a).

4

NARRATION

The Power of Narrators

In the study of social narratives, the concept of narration is important for two reasons. First, it encapsulates the dynamic nature of narrative, pointing at the *process* by which narratives are conveyed (Herman 2009). Second, it invokes the *agents* who are inherent in the communicative acts of producing, consuming, and reproducing narratives. In this sense it puts the spotlight on the narrator role of specific agents and actors, such as political leaders and organizations, which is important to the understanding of the processes that ultimately forge communities (Carr 1986).

The chapter opens with a discussion of the element of narration in the context of social narratives and proceeds towards a more practical orientation regarding this subject. Once again the chapter concludes with a table summarizing the main terms followed by a demonstration of their use in analyzing King George's speech (George VI 1939a).

Narration in Social Narratives

The term *narration* is commonly used to refer to the act or process of producing a narrative, and can be broadly defined as the process of communicating the story. Its original usage emphasized the verbal medium for transmitting messages (Rimmon-Kenan 2002 [1983]: 3). When analyzing social narratives, however, researchers should take into consideration the role of nonverbal communication as well, including visual communication. In this broad sense, narration needs to be understood as encompassing the "entire set of ways in which a story is actually told" (Herman and Vervaeck 2005: 80).

The Study of Narration

As concerns social narratives, it is useful to differentiate between two spheres in which the processes of narration occur. One refers to the social context of the narrative, focusing on the parties responsible for its telling or production. Here the social context is outside of the text; it is extra-textual. In contrast, the second sphere is the narration processes that are part of the narrative text. In this textual sphere, narrators and audience, who are textual figures, are privileged in that their life expectancy is not limited either by the natural cycle of human life or by the average lifespan of an organization. Neither are they subject to temporal and spatial limitations incumbent on entities in reality. Moreover, narrators have the power to create collective voices that extend far beyond face-to-face communication between individuals and endure much longer than the span of an individual's life.

The following sections discuss the element of narration both at the societal and the textual spheres. With respect to the societal sphere, the chapter outlines the communicative dynamic of the narration process that takes place between speakers or writers and audiences. The textual sphere involves the rhetorical mechanisms of telling stories, the range of voices that take part in the process of narration in the social arena, and the various ways in which stories may be told to produce different texts.

The societal sphere: extra-textual narration. The notion of extra-textual narration is premised on the understanding that a story cannot tell itself but rather has to be told (van Hulst 2013: 7). This idea captures the process of communicating the story as a social practice. The term "extra-textual," in this context, encompasses the actors telling the story, including persons, families, firms, organizations, municipalities, and states. It encapsulates the entire communicative process that transpires outside the text, in which a narrative is told and heard, as well as the agents involved in it.

In social science, the terms narration and storytelling can be plausibly regarded as equivalent in meaning. This is especially true for extra-textual narration as the use of storytelling usually emphasizes the practice of telling stories in the context of social interaction (Polletta et al. 2011, Riessman 2008: 7). While narratologists have traditionally favored the term narration, scholars from other fields have, over the years, moved towards the more intuitive concept of storytelling—for example, in sociology (Riessman 2008, 1993), psychology (Nelson 2003, 2004), organizations (Czarniawska 2004, Linde 2009), policy (Yanow 2007), leadership (Grube 2012), and criminology (Shearing and Ericson 1991, van Hulst 2013). The vast majority of these studies embrace extra-textuality in that they are concerned not only with the stories as such but also with the various meanings of storytelling as a social practice.

In the social domain, the identity of storytellers in any given case might seem self-evident. To the extent that social narratives are told by social actors, it might seem commonsensical to assume that storytellers are those who actually speak or write a given narrative text. In actuality, the situation could be much more complex because a social narrative is likely to incorporate a number of different voices belonging to multiple social actors.

Think, for example, of an environmental minister who gives a speech relaying how her ministry has dealt successfully with an environmental crisis. True, the story is being told by a flesh-and-blood human being. But this person wears several hats. She is speaking on behalf of her ministerial office, but also on behalf of the government. Moreover, she may also be speaking on behalf of her state, especially if the issue is of international importance. It is equally possible that she is speaking on behalf of the political party she represents or the coalition to which she belongs. In fact, a speaker or writer of a story may be a vehicle for multiple "voices," even when she does not consciously mean to champion the causes they represent. Speech is a repository for vocabulary, argumentation, ideas, metaphors, and a wide variety of other elements that are rife with presuppositions, assumptions, and perspectives, both explicit and implicit.

A productive discussion of different kinds of speakers can be found in the work of sociologist Erving Goffman (1981). In addressing the question of participation in social interaction, he draws a distinction among three types of speakers: the *animator*, who presents the words, such as a broadcaster; the *author*, who originated the beliefs and sentiments, and composed the words; and the *principal*, whose viewpoint or position is expressed in and through the utterances (Clayman 1992, Goffman 1981). For example, when listening to the news on the radio, the analyst can identify the radio broadcaster as the animator, the person behind the scenes who authored the broadcast (e.g., the news editor), and the station and the senior editor as the principals. Complications may arise if there is, for example, a "hidden" author who leaks an item that then finds its way into the news, or explicit authors and principals who are quoted in the news, and so on.

Members of an audience may also differ in their reception role. In this regard, Goffman's distinction between the addressed and unaddressed recipients of face-to-face communication can be relevant to the study of narration (Goffman 1981, Levinson 1988).[1] However, the rise of new technologies, which have boosted the flow of information, has blurred this distinction, inasmuch as speakers in the public domain can no longer control who their audience is going to be. In other words, in today's world, it is rather difficult to control the flow of information, and the possibility of keeping public messages targeted to a specific audience away from other audiences is limited at best. One field that has been greatly affected by this state of affairs is public diplomacy, namely, the organized attempts by a government to exert as much control as possible over the framing of the country's policy in foreign media (Entman 2008: 89; see also Shenhav, Sheafer and Gabay 2010: 145). It is now very difficult for countries to differentiate the messages directed to their own people from the ones directed to foreign states, a particularly thorny problem when the internal and external messages endorse conflicting interests (Sheafer and Shenhav 2009).

The textual sphere: textual narration. The second aspect of social narration, namely, textual narration, lies within the realm of literary studies, and scholars who are not engaged in this field may be unfamiliar with this notion. It concerns less the actual actors telling a story or the extra-textual social context, and more the process of narration as evidenced in the text. Simply put, *textual narration* refers to the process of communicating the story as documented within the text. In this textual sphere, the text can be viewed as a record of the communicative processes by which the story is being told (see discussion in Herman 2009: 37–9), with the narrators and audience as textual figures.[2]

Scholars of narratology have differentiated between a narrator who is a character in the story, termed *character narrator*, and a narrator who is not a character in the story, that is, a *non-character narrator* (Genette 1980 [1972]: 186, Rimmon-Kenan 2002 [1983]: 92). A character narrator in social narratives commonly figures in cases of self-narration in which a person, an organization, or any agency tells its own story. In these cases a story is often told by a "we" character. This strategy underscores the cyclical nature of social narratives, which are told by a group to the group (see Chapter 1). Take the story of South Africa as told in and by the preamble of the constitution of the state. Rather typically, it opens with the words "We, the people of South Africa." The "we" character then proceeds to relay "our past" and to describe the adoption of the constitution in the course of national events: "We therefore, through our freely elected representatives, adopt this Constitution. . . ." On the whole, the national story is recounted in terms of the "divisions of the past" and the state's future prospects (The Constitution of South Africa 1996). The "we" entity figures both as the narrator of, and as a character in, the story.

Another example of a character narrator is in the story of FC Barcelona as appears on the official website of the soccer club. In the episode describing the threat of closure faced by the club in 1908, its founder Joan Gamper is designated as both a character and a narrator.

> On that famous December 2, 1908, given the collective desertion, Gamper stood up to say "Barcelona cannot and should not die. If there is nobody who wants to try, I shall take full responsibility and look after it in the future."[3]

Despite the obvious differences between the national story of South Africa and the story of the FC Barcelona football club, the two share an important feature: both attempt to establish the legitimacy, validity, and acceptability of their respective narratives by relying on character narrators. The "we" character in South Africa's constitution is a clear case of self-narration that somewhat blurs the sharp distinction between speakers and audience (see Chapter 1). It represents, or endeavors to represent, both the speakers and the audience, as if the nation were addressing itself. The FC Barcelona story legitimates the team through stressing the connection between the founder and the putative immortality of the club.

Note, however, that at the beginning of the FC Barcelona text the story is not conveyed by a character ("On that famous December . . ."). This type of narrator reflects instances where acts of narration are not part of the story, but where the narrator is an outside observer, or cases of an analytic or omniscient narrator (Genette 1980 [1972]).

A heuristically advantageous way to approach narration of a particular story is by asking who tells the story: a third-person narrator can in many instances be identified with a non-character narrator, while a first-person narrator who participates in the events of the story is a character narrator (Phelan and Booth 2005).

Implied author or speakers and implied audiences. As noted by Goffman and discussed earlier, speaker-text-audience relations may be complicated not only by the variety of social actors taking part in communication events, but also on account of different possible types of story ownership, authorship, or responsibility. Differences may also exist in the types of audiences targeted by social texts. But the issue of textual narration involves still further complexities and hence, also, analytical challenges.

It has been argued, for example, that between the real author of a narrative and its narrator there is what is commonly referred to as the *implied author* (Chatman 1978, see discussion in Rimmon-Kenan 2002 [1983]: 87–90). An implied author has been described as "the government consciousness" of a narrative or its "source of norms" (Rimmon-Kenan 2002 [1983]: 87–8, see also Herman 2009: 69). Alternatively, the implied author might be conceived of as a "set of implicit norms" (Rimmon-Kenan 2002 [1983]: 89) that can be abstracted or inferred from the narrative. Neither the implied author nor its *alter ego*, the *implied speaker*, is an "author" or a "speaker" in the concrete sense of these terms. Neither is endowed with agency or appears as a personage in the text. Rather, these constructs can be understood as the values, beliefs, and norms conveyed by the author or speaker.[4]

The idea of implied authors or speakers suggests that it is not always sufficient to study figures or other entities that actually narrate a story, for sometimes implicit voices that direct the narration of stories are no less important. As discussed later, this can be of special interest for critical approaches in studying implicit norms and values emerging from narratives. On a different note, the interrelations between the character narrator and the implied speaker can offer insights into speakers' attempts to convey messages by means of strategic shifts in their narratives between explicit and implicit voices. For example, policy makers who wish to convince their audience that, in handling a certain issue, they exercise caution and deliberation might reinforce this message strategically through the use of symbols, word choice, the choice of issues presented, and various other means. Thus, they may intersperse their speech with words from an appropriate semantic field, such as "calm," "restrained," and "balanced"; report on a certain set of actions, such as discussions, consultations, and examination; and maintain a calm and moderate tone.

While anyone exposed to narrative text may experience, in one way or another, the presence of an implied speaker, a researcher's task can involve characterizing and analyzing the implied speaker and its role in the narrative. As discussed earlier, this can be accomplished by either revealing the narrator's strategy to that effect or by identifying the values and norms projected in the text, on the assumption that a speaker may be more than the person or entity who does the actual speaking. For example, the speaker in Winston Churchill's war speeches is the leader himself,

A researcher can, however, study the implied speaker or author standing behind Churchill. This implied speaker is essentially a collection of norms, values, traditions, ideas, and other elements which are all less concrete than the flesh-and-blood Churchill, but which nevertheless have a "voice" in his public addresses. In other words, it is not only the voice of Churchill, the person, we hear, but also a more abstract, personal voice calling to us through Churchill's speeches.

All in all, when analyzing social narratives, in addition to real, concrete narrators explicitly present in the text in the form of people, groups, institutions, and organizations, etc., researchers can expect to find a variety of abstract narrators. Such implicit narrators play an especially important role in social narratives, which are usually produced through the interaction of multiple speakers and voices.

Parallel to the notions of implied author or implied speaker are those of *implied reader* (Iser 1974) or *implied audience* (Herman 2009). Both can be defined as the intended audience of the implied author (Herman 2009: 187). While it is easy to differentiate between the implied audience and the extra-textual audience, which is the real flesh-and-blood people listening to a text, the distinction between implied audience and the audience intentionally addressed by the narrative is less clear-cut. Nevertheless, social science scholars may find it practicable to differentiate between the audience implicitly appealed to by the text through various linguistic cues and the audience which the text approaches directly through designations such as "you," "we," "our organization," and so on.

In the example above, all the assumptions that can be deduced from Churchill's speeches in regard to the intended audience can be conceived of as the dimensions of an implied audience. Various clues characterize the audience targeted by the speech. For instance, in addition to direct references to his English and American listeners, Churchill characterizes his intended audience both directly, for example, as the "English-speaking world," and more indirectly, by presenting its members as characters in a shared story:

> For the best part of twenty years the youth of Britain and America have been taught that war was evil, which is true, and that it would never come again, which has been proved false.
>
> *(Churchill 1941)*

Churchill further assembles the British and American people under the umbrella of the first-person plural "we"—in contrast to Germany, Japan, and Italy, designated as "they"—and thereby frames the two English-speaking nations as a unified audience:

> We have performed the duties and tasks of peace. They have plotted and planned for war. This naturally has placed us, in Britain, and now places you in the United States at a disadvantage which only time, courage and untiring exertion can correct.
>
> *(Churchill 1941)*

Scholars may choose to approach the investigation of implied audiences by focusing on symbolism and cultural characteristics, which can also be indicative of speakers' assumptions regarding their intended addressees. One example is Churchill's references to psalms: "As long as we have faith in our cause . . . a salvation will not be denied us. In the words of the Psalmist: 'He shall not be afraid of evil tidings. His heart is fixed, trusting in the Lord'" (Churchill 1941). Such an analysis can contribute to an overall assessment of the audience targeted, as it takes into consideration not only concrete or direct references, but also more abstract and complicated elements, which can be no less important.

Critical readers of narrative texts may be particularly intrigued by the power of narration to inculcate values and norms into popular consciousness. A basic premise of critical approaches, such as critical discourse analysis (van Dijk 1993b) or ideological criticism in the study of rhetoric (Foss 2009), is that inequality and power relations are perpetuated through the reproduction of narratives. Crucial for this type of analysis is the role of narration in promoting ideologies and norms via implied speakers, who convey them to imagined audiences.

Table 4.1 displays the main terms in analyzing the element of narration in social narratives as well as their definitions.

TABLE 4.1 Key terms in the analysis of narration

Term	Definition
Narration	the process of communicating the story.
—textual narration	the process of communicating the story as evidenced within the text.
—extra-textual narration	the process of communicating the story as a social practice; this concept encapsulates the communicative process that transpires outside the text.
Narrators	
—textual narrators	
character narrator	cases where a story is narrated by one of its characters.
non-character narrator	cases where a story is not narrated by one of its characters; acts of narration are not part of the story.
implied speaker (or author)	set of implicit norms that can be abstracted or inferred from the text. The intended audience of the implied speaker can be termed as the implied audience.
—extra-textual narrators	
animator	agent who presents the words, such as a broadcaster.
author	agent who originated the beliefs and sentiments, and who composed the words.
principal	agent whose viewpoint or position is expressed in and through the utterances.

Note: some of the concepts in this table are based either fully or partly on the work of other scholars. For citations please refer to these concepts in the text.

Demonstrating the Study of Narration

The study of narration strategies opens promising options for bringing into narrative analysis social and political players who actually do the talking and writing. This kind of investigation can, therefore, be of special interest for researchers who focus on the dynamic of conveying stories, the figures or entities taking part in this process, and fictional or imaginary personages who are both textual characters and narrators.

King George's speech seems to be fertile and inviting ground for demonstrating narration analysis. In the opening part of the speech, discussed in Chapter 3, the communicative position of the speaker is established at the outset. As a character narrator King George addresses every one of his fellow citizens directly, in what feels like a tête-à-tête conversation:

> I send to every household of my peoples, both at home and overseas, this message, spoken with the same depth of feeling for each one of you as if I were able to cross your threshold and speak to you myself.
>
> *(George VI 1939a)*

In the following paragraphs, the King uses the first-person plural—the royal "we," a majestic plural—thereby referring to his own person in a way that is customary for a monarch and at the same time creating a "we" speaker by grouping himself and his hearers together (e.g., "we are at war"; "we have been forced into a conflict"; "we shall prevail"). Toward the end of the speech, King George reverts to the first-person singular of a character narrator, this time also targeting his peoples overseas: "I now call my people at home and my peoples across the seas, who will make our cause their own. I ask them to stand calm" (George VI 1939a). The return to the first-person singular reestablishes the dialogue, which now engages a new audience, the "peoples across the seas." The first-person plural reappears in the concluding part of the speech, when God is mentioned: "But we can only do the right as we see the right, and reverently commit our cause to God." This transition from the first-person-singular narrator, who sends messages to the people, to the first-person-plural narrator, for the more general observations, creates, in a rather sophisticated way, a sense of harmonized multiple voices ("I" and "we"), united in facing a common challenge.

Notes

1. To this distinction Goffman adds one between what he terms *ratified* and *unratified* recipients, that is, the audiences that are officially addressed as opposed to unintended hearers of the message. Although directed toward interpersonal interactions, this distinction is valid and relevant in other social contexts as well. For a clear and detailed explanation and further analysis of Goffman's ideas on this subject, see Levinson (1988).

2. The representation of a living person in a text has been pondered and explored for centuries and can be traced back to the Aristotelian view of *ethos,* mainly in regard to the speaker's personal character understood "by what the speaker says" (Aristotle 2004: 7, Book 1, Part 2).
3. http://arxiu.fcbarcelona.cat/web/english/club/club_avui/mes_que_un_club/mes queunclub_historia.html (accessed October 19, 2014)
4. Note that, if one adopts a very broad conception of implied speakers or audiences, one may simply be analyzing the meanings of texts in dissociation from the communicative processes involved in reading or hearing them. See discussion in Nünning (2005), Rimmon-Kenan (2002 [1983]): 89).

5
MULTIPLICITY
The Proliferation of Social Narratives

It would be an oversimplification to see social narratives only as a means of collective communication in which a group of speakers transfers a message to a group of listeners—like the chorus in a Greek tragedy, speaking to the audience. The proliferation of social narratives cannot be explained solely through the prism of a closed communication system comprised of the speaker-text-audience triad, which may work, for example, for literary texts. Rather, social narratives form a web of communicational events that may occur in different circumstances, take many forms, and involve various actors. The social domain can be seen as an arena for iteration of a communicative situation in which stories, or sometimes versions or parts thereof, are repeatedly told and retold (Kroeber 1992: 9, see also van Hulst 2013, Linde 2009: 74–5, Nelson 2003). This state of affairs presents a challenge to the idea of communication as a single, one-time event involving a speaker and an audience. Instead, we are faced with a dispersion of many communication events in which stories are retold time and again, thereby becoming social entities. This means that "multiplicity" lies at the heart of *social* narratives as a fourth key element. The term refers to the process of repetition and variation through which narratives are reproduced at the societal sphere. It corresponds with the idea that social narratives are embraced by a group and also tell, in one way or another, something about that group (see Chapter 1).

The chapter introduces and elaborates on the notion of multiplicity as an essential facet of social narratives. It then offers practical guidelines to exploring this element. As with the previous chapters, it concludes with a table summarizing the key terms mentioned or discussed in the chapter, followed by the examination of a social narrative through the prism of multiplicity and related concepts. In this chapter the examples are based on two speeches delivered by King George in 1939 on two different occasions.

Multiplicity in Social Narratives

Social narratives are not merely aggregations of stories or other narrative elements. Instead, as will be discussed in this chapter, they are best understood as integrating three communicative elements—speakers, text, and audience—that have proliferated across space and time.

Crucially, a social narrative need not be strikingly original, fascinating, arresting, or dramatic. Its central quality is the impetus to reproduce. Moreover, in the course of their reproduction, social narratives can also be *re-mediated*, that is, transposed from one medium into another (Herman 2009). National stories, for example, appear in various forms—for example, on TV, in the press, in school books, in speeches, and even in national anthems. Such a variety of available forms increases social narratives' potential for multiplicity.

The power of multiplicity. Multiple versions of a narrative can become exceedingly powerful, particularly if they set the norm for a group. When a story or its elements are repeatedly relayed by multiple speakers in a similar manner, alternate versions may be considered as "different" or "odd." A pervasive narrative not only can have an effect on individual members' assessments of and responses to a given situation, it can also be widely perceived as conveying truths, thereby gaining a dominant status over other narratives. To use Catharine MacKinnon's (1996: 235) words, "Dominant narratives are not called stories. They are called reality." In such cases, narratives ultimately become more forceful and influential than the narrators themselves. This dynamic flies in the face of the commonsensical view that narrators have the power to control their stories. Instead, where dominant stories are concerned, that is, stories that are considered compulsory (Shenhav et al. 2014; see also Goddard, Lehr, and Lapadat 2000), it is the stories that often control their narrators, in the sense that the latter cannot even conceive of another way of telling the story, or if they can, will not do so for fear of social sanctions.

The dynamic nature of multiplicity may explain why social narratives are highly adaptable to a changing environment and also why they endure. New variations of events, different characterizations of protagonists, or new settings for the same or similar stories—these are some of the modifications that social narratives undergo on a day-to-day basis and that can ultimately ensure their continued vitality in changing arenas. For example, the Tea Party movement in the United States tells a narrative concerning government along the following lines: "Like the colonists of the Boston Tea Party in 1773, whose rallying cry was 'No taxation without representation,' the modern Tea Party movement also has a cause fundamentally rooted in fairness" (National Coalition of Tea Party Affiliates 2013). A different version of this narrative appears in a speech given on September 4, 2011, during the campaign for the US presidency, by the vice-presidential candidate Sarah Palin:

> President Obama, these people—these Americans—feel that "fierce urgency of now." But do you feel it, sir? The Tea Party was borne of this urgency.

> It's the same sense of urgency that propelled the Sons of Liberty during the Revolution . . . This movement isn't simply a political awakening; it's an American awakening. And it's coming from ordinary Americans, not the politicos in the Beltway . . . We the people, we rose up and we rejected the left's big government agenda. We don't want it. We can't afford it. And we are unwilling to pay for it.
>
> *(Palin 2011)*

The context and medium of the two narratives are different, the text is different, but some major elements of the story are similar, mainly the historical parts that refer to the 1773 Tea Party movement, which are used to frame the current affairs. This demonstrates the multiplicity dynamic at work, shaping a social narrative.

A social narrative's adaptability through multiplicity also accounts for its conservatism, for the same or similar story can reproduce itself time and again, retaining the same or similar assumptions and perspective. Occasionally, however, the changes can be so substantial that the resulting narrative can no longer be plausibly seen as a variation on the old theme, but instead must be treated as a new and different narrative in its own right. Thus, the two texts reproduced earlier would not be identified as two variants of the same narrative if not for their references to the Tea Party movement. In the next section I will elaborate on the question of a boundary between a variation of the same narrative and two different narratives.

A social narrative can bind people together since, as explained earlier, it is not a single narration event, but a series of narration events through which a story or its versions are retold and reheard, time and again, by individuals, organizations, or institutions. The multiplicity concept can help scholars understand how large and lasting groups, such as nations, can instill a feeling of belonging in people who do not know each other and also give them a sense of affinity with those who died long before they were born. It is very likely that members of such groups have been involved in the narration of that story, whether as narrators or as audience, on different occasions. An analogy can be drawn between the dynamic of multiplicity in social narratives and that of the proliferation of Internet *memes*, as discussed by Limor Shifman (2013). Shifman's analysis of the "We Are the 99 Percent" meme presents an interesting case of how the retelling of individual stories can lead to a political story at the macro level.[1] The slogan itself reflects the notion that, in America, 1 percent of the population controls almost all the country's financial wealth. An image of the meme features a person holding a handwritten text containing "her or his gloomy story" culminating in the motto "I am the 99 percent," that is, the 99 percent of society who are not included among the tiny upper-class minority. In consonance with the idea of multiplicity in social narratives, Shifman argues that:

> [It is the] combination of repetition and variation [that] turns the personal to political: Stories about the sick young woman who is unable to afford

medication, the single mom who struggles to provide for her son, and the father who cannot send his daughter to college are reframed as particular cases of the same flawed structure.

(Shifman 2013: 119)

New means for multiplicity. The multiplicity of narratives is not new to humankind, but new technologies, including digital social media, have changed its nature, creating "new narrative norms" (Cornog 2004: 252–3, Polletta et al. 2011: 123) that warrant research attention. So far, I have focused on multiplicity at the textual sphere. However, the means through which narrative texts are reproduced and disseminated are of primary importance for understanding the dynamics of multiplicity—including, most recently, social media enabled through digital means such as the Internet. For example, the distribution of online memes (Shifman 2013), discussed earlier, and the "viral culture" of reproduction and distribution of content have been found to strengthen specific versions of social stories (Wasik 2009), some of which play an important role as forms of persuasion and political participation (Milner 2013, Shifman 2013: Chapter 8).

What is the impact of these new production and reproduction technologies on social narratives? Researchers can assume that the new technologies expedite the transfer of information among people, institutions, and organizations. On the one hand, the rapid duplication and multiplicity of information that take place on almost all levels of society, involving citizens, elites, media, and organized groups, can reinforce the quick integration of particular narratives into popular consciousness. On the other hand, the competition posed by alternative narratives that can also be reproduced at the same speed is increased as well. The result is that intense narrative competitions can come and go very quickly. Importantly, the massive reproduction of existing narratives enabled by digital technologies can strengthen their potential dominance and, at the same time, increase the likelihood of irregularities or mutations in their different versions, which might rapidly gain popularity and perhaps eventually lead to narrative and even social change.

It is not surprising, then, that the effects of digital technologies on social narratives follow a dialectical pattern. New technologies or modes of communication have facilitated the entrenchment of existing narratives, due to massive multiplicity, while at the same time fostering rapid changes and variations in them, as well as the diffusion of new narratives. Within a single society, this dialectic may be manifested in a split between "orthodox" narratives and the voices that challenge them—with the same technologies being used on both sides.

The Study of Multiplicity

The first question that needs to be asked when analyzing the element of multiplicity in a social narrative is what exactly is being multiplied; that is, what *core element* is common to the various multiplied narratives. Narratives can be similar not only in terms of plot types or stories, as discussed in Chapter 2, but also in their more basic component, which I will term "time-theme." This element encapsulates the narrative's take on time and on the subject covered and, as explained later, can be plausibly regarded as the core element of social narratives.

While the idea of time-theme echoes conceptually some of the interpretations of master or metanarratives (see Chapter 2), it differs from it in two important ways. First, the focus is on a concrete textual orientation rather than on broader philosophical, ideological, and sociological issues characteristic of master or metanarratives. Second, the element of time-theme serves as a tool to account for narrative multiplicity in a broader sense, by means of the analogy to fractals explained next.

Fractal geometry as an analogue to social narratives. Conceptualizing the dynamic of multiplicity in social narratives is a complex task, but some possible avenues in this regard are suggested in what follows. In an attempt to understand the dynamic of narrative multiplicity, I draw analogically on fractal geometry. Coined by mathematician Benoît Mandelbrot, the adjectival noun "fractal" derives from the Latin participle fractus (Mandelbrot 1977: 4), meaning "broken or shattered." The Oxford English Dictionary defines a fractal as "a mathematically conceived curve such that any small part of it, enlarged, has the same statistical character as the original" (Oxford English Dictionary Online Edition). Among the various uses of fractals are "to describe nonlinear dynamical systems such as turbulence in fluids, Brownian motion of particles, and geographical coastlines" (Wallin 1989: 137).[2]

A connection between the study of narratives and fractal geometry can be found in the work of literary critic Alexander Argyros. His article "Narrative and Chaos" views a narrative as "a hypothesis about the nature of an existing slice of reality or about the potential consequences of certain variations on a model of the world" (Argyros 1992: 667). Approaching these variations in terms of chaos theory, he argues, sheds light on the "evolutionary adaptation" of narratives, which renders them "simultaneously conservative and innovative" (672). Argyros points out that "the remarkable feature of chaotic systems is their tendency to settle into perdurable patterns, chaotic attractors" (670). These chaotic attractors, Argyros claims, "are fractals—that is, they display similar features at different scales" (666).

A relevant departure point for developing a comprehensive model of the dynamism of multiplicity in social narratives based on the fractal analogue is the following example of the *Mandelbrot set*, the best-known fractal. This is a fractal in which infinite complexity is produced by the iteration of a simple mathematical formula. Figure 5.1 presents two Mandelbrot sets, which I produced with a Java-based program developed by Alfeld (1998).[3] The fractal on the left demonstrates the self-similarity, that is, "the property of having a substructure analogous or identical to an overall structure"(Romanowska-Pawliczek, Pawliczek, and Sołtys 2009: 256) of a big fractal containing small fractals. The similarities contained

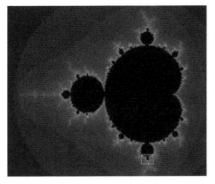 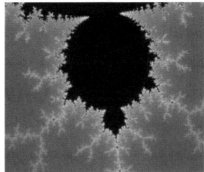

FIGURE 5.1 Two Mandelbrot sets

Note: the fractal on the right-hand side is a magnified view of the portion outlined by the white rectangle on the bottom of the fractal on the left-hand side.
Figures produced with a Java-based program developed by Alfeld (1998).

within that reproduction are shown in the right fractal—a magnified view of the portion outlined in the white rectangle at the bottom of the image on the left.

Zooming in on a portion of the fractal reveals the infinite potential complexity of the Mandelbrot set. As the zooming-in can be performed for each portion of the fractal, an infinite number of new shapes can emerge, usually similar, but not identical, to the entire Mandelbrot set. Taking the above fractal as an analogue for a cluster of multiplied narratives, that is, a group of variations on a similar narrative, may help the researcher to visualize two important characteristics of multiplicity in social narratives.

First, this analogy suggests that behind a multiplied social narrative resurfacing in different versions and mediums lies a simple *core element*—as is the case with the fractal formula (see note 2 in this chapter). In other words, core elements within social narratives contain the potential for new variations, which, in turn, may spawn still more new variations. According to this logic, a necessary condition for the existence of social narratives is their retelling. Think, for example, of nations or religions, both of which are capable of producing powerful social narratives not only to impose the retelling of narratives on their members, but also to create mechanisms that allow for variations of these narratives. Religious or national ceremonies are some of the examples that show the relevance of fractal logic in the transmutation, reproduction, and re-mediation of the social narratives they express.

The second characteristic of multiplicity in social narratives highlighted by the fractal analogue is a possible coexistence of regularity and irregularity. On the one hand, all variations share an important aspect, which is the core element; on the other hand, the process of variation allows for flexibility and adaptability. This quality enables social narratives to perpetuate expected, predetermined, and constant features, while at the same time evolving unexpected new angles.

One advantage of the fractal analogy is that it can help researchers to direct their investigations of multiplicity, seeking to identify the core element of a multiplied narrative. Confronting this challenge inductively, analysts can look for similarities and dissimilarities across narratives that they judge to be based on the same, or similar, stories. A close reading of a text with a focus on repetitions of important elements is one option.[4] More concrete paths for addressing this challenge can also be deduced from the fractal analogue. In what follows I present three such approaches for identifying, tracing, and exploring core elements of social narratives: structural, historical, and exploratory. For the purpose of demonstration, I employ the example of the Zionist narrative from the Declaration of the Establishment of the State of Israel.

Structural approach—time-theme as the core element of narratives. To the extent that social narratives do indeed reproduce in keeping with the fractal logic, a structural approach to analyzing narrative texts pivots on identifying and analyzing core elements in different narratives, focusing on narrative form. As a structural basis of a narrative text, these elements are important to the analysis of social narratives at large, regardless of the specific content of a particular narrative. This is not to say that the content is not factored into the analysis, but only that the focus is on the structure and form of narrative.

The premise underlying the structural perspective is that, while any part of a narrative can be quoted or referenced by other narratives, it is when *core elements* are disseminated that narrative multiplicity takes place. Otherwise, such quotations and references are merely indications of similarities rather than multiplicity.

In line with the fractal analogue, the core element of a multiplied social narrative is expected to reappear in one way or another in all its versions. Tracing such a core element across the multiple versions of a social narrative is a matter of interpretation and evaluation. According to the basic definitions of narrative presented in the Introduction, an important component of the narrative structure is time. If social narratives are indeed formed through the reproduction of their core elements, it is fair to expect these to reference temporal aspects of narrative. Discerning an abstract entity such as a central temporal aspect of a narrative can be challenging. The core element of time is more visible in the parts of texts that bestride the entire temporal framework of the story. Such passages, which in previous studies I have termed *concise narratives* (Shenhav 2005a, see also Chapter 3, note 5), are segments of a narrative text, occasionally a few paragraphs long, that encompass its entire chronological span, or refer to the beginning and end of the narrative. Technically, concise narratives should be relatively easy to identify. A helpful strategy would be to plot the periods of time as referenced in a text and trace graphically the segments that encompass the narrative's entire or almost entire chronological span (see Figure 5.2).

These segments are important for establishing the temporal frame of the narrative. But time is only one of the aspects central to narrative. Narratives are always about occurrences, "something" that happened. Here I contend that

Multiplicity of Social Narratives **63**

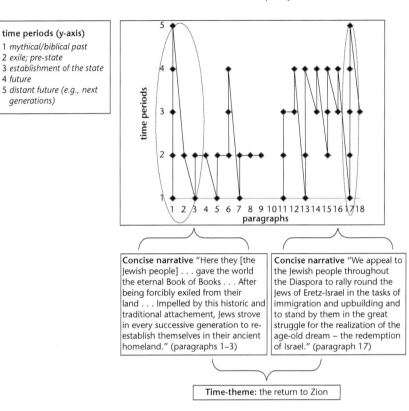

FIGURE 5.2 From temporal dimensions to time-theme: a structural analysis of the Declaration of the Establishment of the State of Israel

sections where a vast stretch of the narrative timeline is compressed into a short segment of text are more likely to convey the broadest topics and ideas of a narrative. The "something" covered in such sections, then, is most likely to be a narrative's major theme. For example, in statements of the kind "we have always been X and will always be Y," the X and the Y are probably major issues in a given narrative, and not secondary or incidental events. Scrutinizing the segments incorporating a narrative's entire or almost entire chronological span could be a helpful technique to study its temporal and thematic identity. Such a time-theme pair represents the narrative's take on time and the subject covered, and can be seen as the way to concretize the idea of the core element of social narratives.[5] Returning to the fractal analogue, if time-theme is indeed an identifiable entity and if it does indeed constitute a narrative's core element, one should expect it to reappear in multiplied narratives.

By way of demonstration, we can perform a time-theme analysis of the Declaration of the Establishment of the State of Israel. In addition to its other functions, the declaration tells the story of the Jewish nation. It starts with a description of the connection between the land of Israel and the Jewish nation, asserting that "ERETZ-ISRAEL [the Land of Israel] was the birthplace of the Jewish people. Here their spiritual, religious and political identity was shaped. . . ." (The State of Israel 1948). The declaration then refers to historic events in the life of the Jewish nation, such as the enforced exile; pioneer immigrants coming to the land of Israel; the First Zionist Congress (1897); the Balfour Declaration (1917); the Holocaust; and the United Nations General Assembly resolution of November 29, 1947, calling for the establishment of a Jewish State in the land of Israel.

Plotting the intersections of text and time on a graph is a useful tool for identifying concise narrative segments, where a time-theme is likely to be found. Figure 5.2 sketches these temporal references. The X-axis reproduces the paragraphs of the declaration, while the Y-axis presents five temporal categories: mythical/biblical past; exile and pre-state era; the modern time—the establishment of the state; future; distant future (see also Shenhav 2005a, 2009).

Let us look at two segments of the declaration that encompass the entire temporal range of the story and thus constitute concise narratives.[6] From a thematic perspective, the first segment (paragraphs 1–3) lays down the "setting" of the narrative. It opens by positioning the land of Israel within an eternal perspective:

> The Land of Israel was the birthplace of the Jewish people. Here their spiritual, religious and political identity was shaped. Here they first attained statehood, created cultural values of national and universal significance and gave to the world *the eternal Book of Books*.
> *(The State of Israel 1948, emphasis added)*

In these paragraphs, the time-theme is the notion of Jews returning to their eternal homeland from exile. It anchors an eternal point of view to the Jewish connection to the land of Israel. The third paragraph refers directly to the idea of the *return to Zion* (in Hebrew: *Shivat Tzion*): "Impelled by this historic and traditional attachment, Jews strove in every successive generation to re-establish themselves in their ancient homeland . . ." (The State of Israel 1948). Although the return-to-Zion motif lacks the succession-of-events criterion to qualify as a story, it still functions as a core element in a constellation of narratives.

As consistency demands, the second segment that references the entire temporal range of the story (i.e., the time-theme) is similar to the first time-theme:

> We appeal to the Jewish people throughout the Diaspora to rally round the Jews of Eretz-Israel in the tasks of immigration and upbuilding and to stand by them in the great struggle for the realization of the age-old dream—the redemption of Israel.
> *(The State of Israel 1948)*[7]

While calling on all Jews "to rally round the Jews of Eretz-Israel"—an appeal that echoes the main theme of return to Zion—this paragraph introduces an additional aspect through the phrase "the redemption of Israel." The concept of redemption points also to a religious orientation of the return-to-Zion time-theme.

All in all, the concept of time-theme in the context of the fractal analogue helps reveal not just the explicit thematic components, but also potentially their possible varieties, which may later reappear in different versions of the narrative.

Historical approach—tracing core elements of narratives. A historical approach to tracking down core elements of social narratives utilizes a longitudinal interpretive analysis of narratives dealing with the same issue.

Tracing a social narrative over time can reveal both its core elements and its changeable aspects. For example, it would be fair to claim that, from a historical perspective, Zionist narratives are tightly linked to the idea or the principle of *the return to Zion*. This expression appears in many different texts, including the biblical books of *Ezra*, *Nehemiah*, and *Psalms* (126), and in several nineteenth and twentieth century texts, where it became a motto for Jewish emigration from the diaspora to the Land of Israel. While, as noted earlier, "the return to Zion" in itself may not qualify as a story (unless, as mentioned in Chapter 1, scholars accept a single continuing event as a sufficient definitional condition *and* understand "the return" as such an event), variations on this idea, phrased, for instance, as "after their exile, the Jews return to their homeland," do constitute stories, definitionally.

The historical approach assumes that tracing social narratives over time can reveal whether they share a theme that makes them variations of the same or similar narrative. It can also be helpful in addressing questions regarding the creation, adaptation, changes, and attrition of social narratives. Combining the structural approach and the historical approach is also possible. In this case researchers can trace time-themes of social narratives over time by utilizing the structural approach.

Exploratory approach—imagining multiplicity. The third direction for studying the role of core elements of social narratives is through evaluating narratives created experimentally by researchers. This is an exploratory method that has hitherto not been used in narrative research. In this approach, the researcher artificially imitates the dynamic of narrative multiplicity through "building" narratives rather than analyzing existing ones.

The exploratory approach is a thought experiment, and should be seen as such. By means of this imagining process, researchers create and study, *inter alia*, potential changes and deviations in social narratives. In line with the concept of time-theme as the core element in the multiplicity of social narratives, the idea behind this approach is to explore the potential of time-themes to produce narratives. In practice, our task as scholars here is, first, to become exploratory narrators and, then, to evaluate the narratives we have created.[8] The exploratory

TABLE 5.1 Key terms in the analysis of multiplicity

Term	Definition
Multiplicity	the process of repetition and variation through which narratives are reproduced at the societal level.
Fractal/fractal analogue	a mathematically conceived curve such that any small part of it, enlarged, has the same statistical character as the original (Oxford English Dictionary Online Edition). The fractal analogue is used in this chapter to describe the multiplicity of social narrative.
Core element	a crucial element common to multiplied narratives, making them variations of a similar narrative. In light of the fractal analogue, it is equivalent to the formula that generates the fractals.
Time-theme	the concretization of core element in social narratives. The time-theme encapsulates the narrative's take on time and subject.
Concise narrative	a segment of a narrative text that encompasses its entire chronological span; alternatively, a part of the text that refers to the beginning and end of the narrative. Time-themes are likely to appear in concise narratives.

approach affords the opportunity to analyze differences and similarities between narratives based on the reproduction of time-themes. Its main drawback, however, lies precisely in its being a thought experiment. As the analysis is not based on attested data, its evidentiary status is compromised and it might be deemed speculative. Still, this strategy may shed light on hypothetical questions such as: What kind of narratives can emerge based on a specific time-theme? Or how can changes in a particular time-theme affect the social narratives created around it? Let us take the latter question as an example. Technically it can be addressed by taking a time-theme of interest and writing down alternative narratives based on it, then making some changes in that time-theme and writing down other possible narratives based on the amended version, then making new changes, and so on and so forth. This process may help to develop educated assumptions regarding possible future changes in a social narrative and also to foresee possible effects of a change when constructing new narratives.

The main terms and techniques for analyzing multiplicity in social narratives are presented in Table 5.1.

Demonstrating the Study of Multiplicity

The idea of multiplicity may lead researchers beyond the frame of a single narrative text. One way of addressing the process of textual reproduction—be it via radio broadcasts, newspapers and other publications—is by studying a narrative text as represented in its historical or artistic variants. For King George's wartime address (George VI 1939a), the latter can be the dramatic scene at the end of the film *The King's Speech*.[9]

A possible path for analyzing multiplicity in this narrative would be to study narrative change by tracing the time-theme and analyzing the narrative in light of this core element. The historical approach adds a longitudinal perspective, and is therefore useful in probing questions of narrative changes. The following very brief demonstration combines both these approaches.

In King George's speech, the first two paragraphs encompass the entire chronological span of the narrative—from the earliest times (referenced by the statement, "In this grave hour, perhaps the most fateful in our history, I send to every household of my peoples . . . this message") to the previous war, to the attempts to prevent the current war, to the present state of being at war, to future events: "For we are called, with our allies, to meet the challenge of a principle which, if it were to prevail, would be fatal to any civilised order in the world" (George VI 1939a, paragraphs 1 and 2). This concise narrative, which starts in a historical past and ends by describing a hypothetical future catastrophe in the event that Britain should not enter the war, is a clear-cut example of a justification strategy. The main theme of this section is the common wartime premise that a war is inescapable: "We have been forced into a conflict." This theme is embedded in a historical temporal perspective ("this grave hour") and in the communicative context of the king sending his "message." Interestingly, the time-theme in this case incorporates, on a metalevel, the act of communication between the king and his people in the face of an imminent war. Only at the end of the speech, well outside the boundaries of the concise narrative discussed earlier, does the prospect of a happy ending materialize: "we shall prevail."

The limited scope of this discussion does not allow for an in-depth, comprehensive, longitudinal analysis of narrative changes throughout the war period. It is, however, possible to demonstrate the use of concepts presented in this chapter by adducing another speech by King George VI (1939b), delivered several months after the first address. The time-theme in the later speech (1939b) appears to be somewhat different from that in the earlier one (1939a). It is still concerned with the confrontation with the enemy and incorporates a communication act, but two important changes are noteworthy. First, the focus of the later speech, as evidenced by its concise narrative sections, is not on communication but on national unity; second, the idea of prevailing over the enemy in the future is now part of the time-theme:

> [I]t is the tragedy of this time that there are powerful countries whose whole direction and policy are based on aggression and the suppression of all that we hold dear for mankind. It is this that has stirred our peoples and given them a unity unknown in any previous war. We feel in our hearts that we are fighting against wickedness, and this conviction will give us strength from day to day to persevere until victory is assured.
>
> *(George VI 1939b)*

The theme of unity-cum-victory subsequently reappears in another concise narrative:

> Such is the spirit [of freedom] of the Empire; of the great Dominions, of India, of every Colony, large or small. From all alike have come offers of help, for which the Mother Country can never be sufficiently grateful. Such unity in aim and in effort has never been seen in the world before [. . .] Let us remember this through the dark times ahead of us and when we are making the peace for which all men pray.
>
> *(George VI 1939b)*

It is not argued here that the time-theme of the first is totally at odds with that of the second. However, the time-theme of the latter, which combines the aspects of unity and future victory, reflects an evolution of the prevailing wartime social narratives. Analyzing this gradual change in the time-theme is an example of the concepts and approaches discussed here for studying evolutionary adaptations of or changes in social narratives.

Notes

1. The term *meme* can be defined as "small units of culture that spread from person to person by copying or imitation" (Shifman 2013: 2).
2. Jean Baudrillard (1993: 5–6) uses the idea of fractal (or viral or radiant) as a pattern of values that denotes "a lack of point of reference" (see also Gane 2000 and Wade 2014).
3. I wish to thank Professor Peter Alfeld who was kind enough to give me permission to use the image produced by his program. The Mandelbrot set is generated by a simple formula often expressed as $z = z^2 + c$. The program is publicly available at: http://www.math.utah.edu/~pa/math/mandelbrot/mandelbrot.html (accessed March 8, 2014).
4. Close reading can be defined as "the mindful, disciplined reading of an object with a view to deeper understanding of its meanings" (Brummett 2009: 3, 25).
5. To some extent, the concept of time-theme is similar to that of chronotope, coined by Bakhtin (1981) to refer to "time spaces" in the context of literary criticism. Bakhtin maintains that "chronotope" captures the "intrinsic connectedness of temporal and spatial relationships that are artistically expressed in literature" (84). In social narratives, however, the element of time may or may not be connected to space as a major theme: social narratives can have other pivotal themes as well.
6. From a narrative perspective, these segments are equally important. From historical and political perspectives, it makes sense to claim that paragraph 11, which constitutes a declarative speech act ("[we] hereby declare the establishment of a Jewish state"), is of greater importance.
7. The original Hebrew of the English "age-old dream" is literally translated as "the aspiration of all generations."
8. To avoid a possible cognitive overload these two tasks can be divided among several researchers.
9. In the case of King George's speech, the multiplicity mechanism is discernible and seems to be quite direct. In addition to reports in various newspapers, the day following the actual speech, *The Times* (1939) announced that the UK information ministry planned to print its copy and send it to every household in the UK.

6
NORMATIVE PERSPECTIVES IN THE STUDY OF SOCIAL NARRATIVES

In the previous chapters, I have examined four key elements in the study of social narratives: story, text, narration, and multiplicity. This chapter moves away from that conceptual and methodological orientation to a discussion of the growing literature that connects the study of narrative to a variety of normative questions. Normative approaches in the study of narratives cover a wide range of issues, from the researcher's position to the role of social narratives in influencing the rules of society. The chapter addresses a number of normative perspectives in regard to each of those four key elements.

First, the chapter touches on the longstanding debate about the relation between *stories* and "social reality" and the moral and ideological implications of this debate for social-narrative research. Next, the concept of intertextuality is discussed, in the sense of one text appearing in another text, as well as its role in power relations within society. The section that follows is devoted to the theoretical and societal questions regarding the narrators of social stories. Among the issues covered are strategies employed by socially marginalized narrators to tell their stories and the means through which narrators can be empowered. The chapter concludes with a discussion of the interrelations among multiplied narratives in the social domain, based on three main models: a dominant narrative, competing narratives, and narrative proximity.

Story and Reality: A Normative Perspective in the Study of Story

The study of stories in the social domain cannot be dissociated from scholars' normative perspectives concerning a number of issues. Probably the most fundamental of these in narrative research concerns the relationship between story and social reality. A frequently explored question in this regard is whether the former is or can be a "true" representation of the latter. Over the years, scholars have approached this question from many different angles (e.g., Ankersmit 2005, Carr 1986, Maynard-Moody and Musheno 2006: 322–3, Polkinghorne 1988, Riessman 1993: 22–3, Shenhav 2006, Widdershoven 1993). As discussed later, it is also a relevant issue in nonscholarly arenas.

Although I see this matter as a general concern applicable to all areas of narrative research, the question relating to the truthfulness of a story can best be explained and concretized using the example of historiography. As put by philosopher David Carr, it is traditionally believed or understood that narrative histories claim to tell us what really happened (although this is a contested claim in contemporary theorizing, as discussed later); in equal measure, however, it is believed or understood that real events "simply do not hang together in a narrative way, and if we treat them as if they did we are being untrue to life" (Carr 1986, 117). Note that these diametrically opposed points of view—that stories can accurately represent social realities and that they cannot—both concede that stories do not just spring into being but are told by someone (whether an individual, a group, or many groups). In other words, the debate is not between those who regard a story as a full and true representation of reality, on the one hand, and others who challenge the notion of truth in any narrative text, on the other. Few, if any, scholars nowadays hold the rather naïve view that stories—even what we call "true" stories—are a complete accurate reflection of reality. Instead, the debate is really over the extent to which stories reflect "social realities" (for a more nuanced discussion, see Polkinghorne 1988: 67–8, see also Ankersmit 2005). This is a philosophical matter that, in my opinion, cannot be resolved. But it is possible to outline the main approaches to the matter and discuss their normative and methodological implications.

Two main approaches can be identified. First, some scholars impute to narratives a substantial ability to reflect reality based on the idea that stories, like reality, are structured along a chronological axis. Paul Ricoeur is often cited in support of this argument, in consequence of his claim that "time becomes human to the extent that it is articulated through a narrative mode" (Ricoeur 1984: 52). Ricoeur posits a reciprocal relation between narrativity and temporality, conceiving of temporality as the "structure of existence that reaches language in narrativity," while he conceives of narrativity as "the language structure that has temporality as its ultimate referent" (Ricoeur 1980: 169). Seen in this light, narrative does in some ways represent the lived experience of time.

The second approach conceives of stories as produced by humans so as to help them to cope with a nonnarrative reality. Among the foremost advocates of this theoretical model is Hayden White (1980), who asserts that the historian's predilection for narrative forms is rooted in the human desire to endow reality with coherence and meaning. Imposing narrative structures on reality, according to White (1980: 18), is a way "to moralize the events." Note that White's definition of narrative differs from the one suggested in this volume: his position appears to be rooted in the premise that narrative requires causal and structural organization, that is, a beginning, middle, and end. Perhaps the most unambiguous rendering of this second approach belongs to philosopher Louis Mink (1987), who comments aphoristically that "stories are not lived, but told" (60). In a similar vein, Elliott Mishler (1995) contends that "we do not find stories; we make stories" (117). On the whole, however, the view of stories as human constructions is fundamentally different from the one that attributes narrative properties to reality.

The preference for one approach over the other might be rooted in individual intuitions, beliefs, or ideology. For example, if scholars, or indeed laymen, posit that a story is a truthful representation of reality, they thereby bestow on its narrator(s) the prerogative of vetoing other stories on account of their allegedly inadequate representations. Privileging a particular story as the true representation of historical, social, or political events would obstruct other narratives from challenging it or suggesting an alternate perspective. Looming in the background, meanwhile, is the question of who is authorized to create these "real" stories. But assuming that stories are immanently inventions can undermine people's beliefs in the truth of national stories, sacred texts, or history. This particular dilemma transcends the debate over the nature of stories and touches on a more fundamental question regarding the role of reality and truth in social life. The choice of one approach over the other may be a function of an individual's beliefs, values, or intuition regarding questions of relativism or the truthfulness of historical, sacred, or another kind of social narratives. This choice can also depend on one's state of mind: whether one is able to cope with uncertainty or whether one wishes to exist in a more definitive and "solid" state of consciousness.

A researcher's position regarding the potential of stories to reflect reality may lie on a continuum between these two diametrically opposite poles. At one end is the assumption that stories cannot represent any aspect of reality, that is, that they are inherently fictional. An intermediate point would be to acknowledge a story's capacity for episodic representation, in the sense of rendering discrete events accurately, but not their chronological or other ordering. Further along the continuum is the capacity for chronological representation, that is, an assumption that chains of events in stories can capture sequences of events in reality. Next in order is the capacity for accurate representation of other connections between events: the assumption that stories are capable of representing not only the events and temporal relations between them, but also other types of connection, such as causality. And at the other end is the capacity for full representation, including not just the story itself but also all other narrative elements. This choice is tantamount to a belief that there are, or can be, narratives that mirror reality fully, a position that may appear untenable for many scholars (Shenhav 2006).

Beyond ideological and moral significance, this dilemma has methodological implications for narrative analysis. For example, the position taken in this regard can determine whether analysis will attempt to assess stories by comparison with an "external" reality or will focus instead on internal modes of the construction of stories.

So far, I have discussed the story–reality question mainly in representational terms. However, to the extent that people think and communicate through stories, the issue of representation cannot be dissociated from the question whether stories form and change social reality. If indeed, as argued in the Introduction, stories contain repertoires of reactions to social situations that can guide people's actions. This particular role cannot be ignored in discussing the story–reality relationship. Importantly, besides the philosophical dilemma of whether or to what extent stories are lived and not only told, it can give rise to a view that sees stories and "reality," or "life," as engaged in the process of mutual imitation. This approach is in line with a claim advanced by Jerome Bruner (1987), who studies narratives in psychology, that "[n]arrative imitates life, [while] life imitates narrative" (13).

What does Bruner (1987) mean when he says that life imitates narrative? From a psychological perspective, "life" is "constructed by human beings through active ratiocination, by the same kind of ratiocination through which we construct narratives" (13). But could this be possible in the social domain as well? In some respects and on some occasions, this question can be answered in the affirmative because a story may become a model or script for human behavior. Furthermore, people may adjust their expectations as concerns their lives to various elements of a story, such as a happy ending. They may structure their social reality or their expectations thereof according to the stories they read and the movies they see (see discussion in Czarniawska 2004, Sarbin 2004, Zilber 2009). In his article "Life Is Not a Dramatic Narrative," Alan Dershowitz (1996) analyzes an episode from the O. J. Simpson murder trial, in which he served as an adviser for the defense team. He discusses the judge's ruling concerning whether the prosecutor could relay to the jury the defendant's alleged dream that he would kill Nicole Brown, the victim. The prosecutor, in supporting her argument, cited the Walt Disney song "A Dream Is a Wish Your Heart Makes." Dershowitz uses this example to show how poetic conventions, in this case taken from a song in a children's film, can be internalized and understood as "real" even in a court setting. Even though, as Dershowitz (1996: 104) maintains, in real life "dreams do not come true; [t]hey are not even wishes," his analysis demonstrates how "real life" can be confused with, and thus affected by, fictional stories.[1]

As this case illustrates, people's lives can be guided by their interpretations of the stories to which they are exposed. It is therefore feasible to add to the scholarly understanding of the relationship between narrative and "reality" the element of mutual formation and change, which stresses the interaction between "life," or "reality," and the stories that humans create. This view implies that stories should not be seen as inert mirror images of life, but as active participants in the processes of mutual imitation, which the story and "reality" accomplish through representation, interpretation, and formation.

In sum, an analysis of the relationship between story and reality can never be free from value judgments, standpoints, or outcomes. Stories can be understood as human fictions, as modes of expression capable of fully representing reality, or as located somewhere between these two poles—but the researcher's choice of a position on this issue is always fraught with consequences for the particular analysis. Yet, the story–reality dilemma can also be addressed in a rather different way that does not involve a choice of one or the other extreme. This view emphasizes the process of mutual imitation that obtains between social stories and social realities, such that each element both shapes and is shaped by the other. This interactive approach is centered on the theoretical premise that occurrences are translated or transformed into the storyworld, and vice versa. This kind of imitation can never be perfect or static; stories and society can either sustain and reinforce each other, or create a dynamic of change. Possibly it is this intersection between stories and society, as well as the reciprocity of their interrelations, that makes social narratives so powerful.

Domination and Social Texts: A Normative Perspective in the Study of Text

The material nature of texts (see Chapter 3) makes them vulnerable to political domination and social control. While the interpretive process whereby individuals reconstruct stories from texts takes place within the human mind and is therefore difficult to regulate, the text itself can be controlled given that it is embedded in material, physical elements. A concrete, tangible, and somewhat brutal way of controlling texts is through censorship. A subtler, yet also more complicated means of social control is ordering texts into hierarchies. States employ a variety of strategies to create hierarchies of texts. This can be carried out through recording, documenting, and storing texts, for instance, by using protocols, digitization, and archives; through various mechanisms of their distribution to audiences; or through ranking texts in terms of importance. This process is often institutionalized. Governments invest resources to document the proceedings of certain forums, such as parliamentary discussions, and to archive them in public libraries or online, while neglecting to record discussions in other forums—which, as a consequence, are lost or forgotten. States also control, at least partly, dissemination capabilities such as print, radio, TV, internet, and education systems. Legitimating and delegitimating possible speakers is yet another way of creating hierarchies.

Competition over the means of disseminating texts is at the center of technological advancement. Whereas modes of production are important for the material control over the content of texts, actors can achieve dominance over the social arena with their narratives in other ways, for example, by framing them as "true" or "common sense," or by lying about their truthfulness. The strength of dominant texts cannot be evaluated merely on the basis of visible public indicators, as explained by Scott:

> The dominant never control the stage absolutely, but their wishes normally prevail. In the short run, it is in the interest of the subordinate to produce a more or less credible performance. . . . It is in precisely this public domain where the effects of power relations are most manifest, and any analysis based exclusively on the public transcript is likely to conclude that subordinate groups endorse the terms of their subordination and are willing, even enthusiastic, partners in their subordination.
>
> *(Scott 1990: 4)*

Accordingly, in studying the discourse of the powerless, Scott suggests focusing on what he calls "hidden transcripts," in the sense of offstage discourses. In addition to the social status of narrators and listeners, narratives can be endowed with power through the interrelationships between various texts, embodied by the idea of *intertextuality*. A key concept in discourse analysis and in the study of literature, it refers to the presence of one text in another. Literary critic Julia Kristeva (1970), who coined the term, claims that "all texts are inherently intertextual" (Moraru 2005: 257; for a narrative analysis that applies the concept of intertextuality, see Linde 2009: Chapter 8). Quotations, allusions, metaphors, direct or indirect references, and even structural similarities produce a web of connections among texts. Intertextuality can also be tapped by following the ongoing dialogue texts have with other texts and, in much broader and abstract terms, with society and culture as a whole (Bakhtin 1981).

Intertextuality is a good way to account for power relations between texts regardless of the role of social actors. It can show how the power of texts can be rooted in projecting "common sense," in using "accepted" terminology, or simply in being "mainstream."

The Power to Narrate: A Normative Perspective in the Study of Narration

Influential narrators—those who can be regarded as either bringing new narratives to the social domain or as changing its narrative trends—can have considerable control over important aspects of society, sanctioning events, endorsing key players, and establishing causal relations. While anyone can be a narrator in the social domain, only very few achieve the status of influential narrators. Borrowing Goffman's terminology, presented in Chapter 4, people usually participate in social narration as *animators* of existing narratives. For example, by virtue of singing a national anthem (provided it tells a story), people become animators of this social narrative. By the same token, people telling their colleagues a story that is subsequently canonized as part of the company's "mythology" are likewise animators rather than *authors* who originated the story.

But how can one become an influential narrator? In other words, how can one succeed in bringing new narratives into being, changing existing social narrative trends, or initiating new ones? In light of the basic communication process that occurs when a speaker tells a story to an audience, this question can be discussed in relation to three elements: the tellability of stories, the characteristics of the speakers, and the characteristics of the audience.

The tellability of stories. A story's tellability refers to the qualities that enable a story to be told, and told well (Baroni 2011, Herman 2009, Labov 1972, Schmid 2010, van Hulst 2013). The underlying idea is that good stories make good narrators. There is no rule of thumb as to which story is more tellable and which is less so. In social narratives, it is obviously not only a matter of gripping drama or an interesting plot, as might be the case in fiction, but also of the social importance of a story: how relevant its topic is to current social debates. Needless to say, the tellability of stories changes across societies and over time.

Cases of dominant stories (see later discussion) show the great power stories can bestow on their narrators. Since dominant stories are used by social actors to sustain and perpetuate their own status in society, the promoters of dominant stories enjoy narratological as well as social advantages. The reason is that, by gaining dominance, such stories determine the "safe" boundaries of conventional, mainstream discourse, rendering other stories vulnerable to being treated as odd, different, deviant, or wrong.

Rather paradoxically, when new stories do not outright reject the dominant stories but rather clash with some of their aspects or perceptions, they may reinforce at least parts of dominant stories by making them more palatable to the mainstream audience. An insightful demonstration of this dynamic is Sparks' (1997) analysis of the story of Rosa Parks, an African American civil rights activist who, in 1955, resisted bus segregation, subsequently becoming a symbol of the civil rights movement. Sparks claims that telling a story in no way guarantees that it will be heard, and that less powerful actors often tell stories that the more powerful simply ignore. She shows that to convey a message against racism, Rosa Parks was characterized as a "courageous heroine" whose dissidence, however, "was performed in a manner that did not conspicuously threaten traditional gender norms, sexuality norms, or class norms" (99). Sparks notes that a few months before Parks's act of protest, a younger woman was arrested on similar charges, but community leaders decided not to take up her case when she "turned out to be pregnant out of wedlock" (99). By contrast, Rosa Parks's more conventionally acceptable image increased the chances that her message about race would be heard, while at the same time reinforcing other dominant, accepted stories (e.g., about marriage and childbirth).

The characteristics of the speakers. The evaluation of tellability is often dissociated from the narrator her- or himself and the way the story is told. When it comes to the social domain, however, one cannot ignore the role of the narrator's ethos or status as a parameter determining whether the narrative seems credible and influential. Whether the speaker is a flesh-and-blood individual in the extratextual context or a character embedded in the text, his or her social status and power affect the amount of attention accorded the story by the audience. In some cases, the speaker's impact may also partly depend on whether he or she controls the means of the production of narrative texts (see discussion in Scott 1990).

Another factor that determines a narrator's power relates to the effect of narration and the rhetorical means employed by narrators. Persuasive and inspiring orators, such as Martin Luther King, Jr. or Winston Churchill, use rhetorical power to change the long-standing stories through which people are used to conceptualizing their worlds.

The characteristics of the audience. Societies and groups may differ in their acceptance of new social narratives. As they maneuver their way around prevailing norms and popular opinions, narrators cannot escape the realization that introducing new narratives to the social domain may bring not only benefits, but sometimes also sanctions.

It seems fair to assume that audiences will not throw themselves into the arms of every new social narrator.[2] In this context, for new narrators, an attempt to challenge dominant stories may prove an extremely trying experience. They have to confront not only the stories as such but also the *comme d'habitude* narrators who customarily tell social stories. In the contexts where the audience is characterized by aggressive and intolerant conservatism, we can expect a hostile reaction to the construction of new narratives or to attempts to deconstruct or reconstruct existing narratives. It is also important to note that hostility can be directed against the dominant story, that is, against reinforcing existing dominant narratives, for example, in the event of an aggressively antiestablishment audience that disdains any support of stories told by "the government."

The question of the extent to which a society will accept new narrators has important normative implications. A society that refuses to accept new narrators bearing new narratives might be in danger of expanding and exacerbating the discrepancies between the stories it tells about itself and the day-to-day experiences of rank-and-file citizens. In the context where society changes but its entrenched narratives remain unchanged, the latter might be either gradually delegitimized or forcibly inculcated into popular consciousness through indoctrination or through policies based on the assumption that the obsolete narratives are still valid and must be put into practice.[3]

The question of whether a group or a society should be hospitable to new narrators is essentially normative. To evaluate the extent to which a given society is open to new narrators and new stories, one would need to probe the "climate" surrounding the construction, reconstruction, and destruction of social narratives. Across societies, this climate may vary in terms of tolerance or hostility toward narrative changes.

Narrative mobility. Researchers can utilize the three perspectives discussed—the tellability of stories, the characteristics of the speakers, and the characteristics of the audience—to evaluate the narrative mobility of a given society, in the sense of its tolerance to new narrators and narratives. As a working assumption, researchers can posit that every society or group finds an equilibrium point between accepting and rejecting new social narratives, and empirically evaluate this equilibrium as well as the possibility of its loss.

Multiplicity and Relations among Narratives: A Normative Perspective in the Study of Multiplicity

Chapter 5 examined the dynamic of multiplicity in the variations of a single narrative. Multiplicity, however, can also be manifested in the relations among different narratives. From a societal perspective, the multiple versions of different narratives embraced by people form the warp and woof of human society.[4] Understanding widespread beliefs concerning the relations among narratives may be important for appreciating the internal conflicts or ambivalences people experience in their day-to-day lives.

We may distinguish among three major types of relations between social narratives: *dominant-story* relations, *competing-stories* relations and *story-proximity* relations (Shenhav et al. 2014). For the sake of simplicity, I will focus on the aspect of story in these relations, although a more in-depth analysis can incorporate other narrative elements as well.

Dominant Story. A dominant social story can be defined as a story that is embraced by a group and that its members consider normal or desirable or perceive as compulsory (Goddard, Lehr, and Lapadat 2000; Shenhav et al. 2014). While the usual understanding is that dominant stories eliminate other stories, this is not obligatory. Dominant stories can coexist with other social stories. That is best understood if the researcher considers the nature and implications of dominance. First, dominance may assume either benign or hostile forms, and this presumably affects the tolerance of those who embrace prevailing stories toward those who adopt different stories. Second, there is the question of how a story becomes dominant: whether it is *imposed* by elites or is accepted due to its popularity among the public.

Whichever is the case, a dominant story usually overshadows, marginalizes, or excludes other stories (e.g., Krebs forthcoming a, Krebs forthcoming b, Krebs and Lobasz 2007). In doing so, it presents a certain sequence of events and the characters involved therein as the "real," the "normal," or "common sense" manner of seeing social reality. The endurance of dominant stories is premised on the willingness of a group to view its own existence as centered around a single story. For example, fundamentalist groups are more likely to adopt a single, exclusive story. Overall, some people find it more difficult than others to live by one main story, and some are more open than others to changes in leading stories. It is also possible to differentiate between social issues that call for a single (dominant) story and those that are amenable to diversification.

In all cases, the existence of a dominant story presupposes a common cognitive element that is shared by members of a group who adhere to the particular story the group advocates or to similar versions thereof. This view evokes the concept of social cognition, which has been defined as "socially shared representations of societal arrangements, groups and relations, as well as mental operations such as interpretation, thinking and arguing, inferencing and learning, among others" (van Dijk 1993b: 257). The concept of social cognition makes it theoretically possible to tie together individual and collective levels of society (van Dijk 1993b: 257). As such, it has become a pivotal concept linking dominance and discourse in the theoretical framework of critical discourse analysis (van Dijk 1993b), and it is relevant for understanding the establishment of dominant stories in the social domain. For a multiplied story to become dominant, it must be part of the social cognition of its largest or most influential group. This dominance may hold true for various levels of analysis. For example, to the extent that there is such a thing as "organizational cognition"—characteristic, for example, of a police force, elite military units, corporate firms, NGOs, and governmental agencies—a story could become dominant in one of these, as well.

Competing stories. Some social stories, such as national stories, are constantly vying for hegemony in the social domain, such that the establishment of one necessarily entails the repudiation of its competitors (e.g., Patterson and Monroe 1998). From a theoretical point of view, the focus is on the struggle between stories for hegemony or control, an idea that is occasionally framed in terms of counternarratives (Andrews 2004). Counternarratives can sometimes be marginal, for example, in the case of a small political movement challenging the government, but they can also be very powerful, as in national politics where two different stories compete for political control (Shenhav et al. 2014).

Proximity between stories. The proximity relationship refers to the degree of similarity between story versions. The concept of proximity presupposes that similarities or dissimilarities in the stories people embrace about their group should influence or reflect their behavior and perception in a range of areas. For example, Sheafer, Shenhav, and Goldstein (2011) found that, for most parties, voting behavior in the 2009 Israeli election was significantly affected by the proximity between individual voters' stories and political parties' stories.

The assumption behind this approach is that the greater the proximity between stories, the greater the likelihood that their proponents will coexist in relative harmony (Sheafer, Shenhav, and Goldstein 2011, Shenhav et al. 2014).

The study of proximity relations between stories can proceed in various directions. One could explore, for example, how individuals or groups of people who rally round a certain story relate to other individuals or groups who adhere to a different story. Alternatively, it is possible to focus on the relations among the stories *per se* rather than among individuals and groups who champion them. Whichever the case, the proximity perspective adds nuance to the study of relations among multiple social narratives.

Normative Dilemmas in the Study of Social Narratives

This chapter has examined some of the growing literature that focuses on normative or value-related questions in the study of social narratives. Even a brief look at such issues reveals a wide variety of directions to approach this subject. The long-standing and much discussed question regarding the relation between story and reality has important implications for the researcher's stance—a question that, as explained above, is normative in nature. The issue of intertextuality bears mostly on the narrative text, while questions regarding the status of a narrative or the relations among multiplied social narratives (involving such factors as dominance, competition, and proximity) have more to do with audiences and social contexts. The earlier discussion by no means implies that social-narrative research must necessarily focus on normative questions. However, any scholar engaged in such research should be aware of its numerous normative aspects and make an informed decision whether or not to address them in a given study.

Notes

1. Dershowitz's claim accords with the literature analyzing the processes in which fairy tales both represent and shape the way individuals and societies perceive the world (e.g., Zipes 1994; Bettelheim 1976).
2. See, for example, Neuman, Just, and Crigler (1992) on how people actively and critically interpret news stories.
3. An example can be Suny's (1988) analysis of the tensions between USSR official state ideology that "droned on about the harmony between the party and the people" and dissidents who spoke on the conflict between public authority and individual consciousness (432).
4. On the political ramifications of these multiple options in today's society, see Ezrahi (2012).

7
ANALYZING SOCIAL NARRATIVES

Whether concentrating on story, text, narration, or multiplicity, a researcher of social narratives is placed in a situation fraught with inherent tensions. The nature of the analysis compels him or her to inhabit simultaneously three different "worlds": the storyworld of the narrative studied; the context in which the story was created or is being told, or both; and the research task-governed scholarly universe.[1]

To gain a first-hand experience of the three "worlds," imagine that you are researching national identity in Andorra, and you have found the following lyric from the state's national anthem, which you think might bear upon your study:

> The great Charlemagne, my Father, liberated me from the Saracens,
> And from heaven he gave me life of Meritxell the great Mother.
> I was born a Princess, a Maiden neutral between two nations.
> I am the only remaining daughter of the Carolingian empire
> Believing and free for eleven centuries, believing and free I will be.
> The laws of the land be my tutors, and my defender Princes!
> And Princes my defender!
>
> *(Andorra 1921)*

Think of a question that you would like to address regarding this text and read the verses again. Here is a possible question: consider the significance of the female first-person narrator in this anthem ("I was born a Princess"), as opposed to the typical "we" narrator of national narratives. At the same time, do your best to immerse yourself in the events referred or alluded to in the text: the story of the princess, her father, and the princes. And now think about contexts in which this story is likely to be told. These may include a variety of ceremonies that customarily feature the singing of national anthems, the historical events metaphorically alluded to in the lyric, or any other sociohistorical context. If you find this particular text too opaque, go back to Chapter 3 and reread the first paragraph of King George's war address (1939) in light of a research question of your own choosing, keeping in mind the sociohistorical context in which the speech was delivered—all the while immersing yourself in the events mentioned in the text.

It is possible that, while reading the paragraph in light of the question you set out to analyze, you experienced some of the three different "worlds" described earlier: the storyworld, the social context, and the analytical scholarly assignment. This kind of tripartite state of being is, I believe, part and parcel of any sensitive analytical reading of narrative texts, and it is invaluable in narrative analysis. The concepts and methods outlined in this and the preceding chapters are mostly geared toward analysis but are nevertheless helpful for partaking of and sustaining this entire tripartite existence.

In this final chapter I suggest a practical means to shift from the discrete elements of narrative, discussed in the preceding chapters, to a comprehensive approach that can utilize the methods and theoretical guidelines these chapters present.

Analyzing Narratives—Thin and Thick Perspectives

The preceding chapters have elaborated on four narrative elements, respectively: story, text, narration, and multiplicity. With the help of these concepts, I have endeavored to develop a theoretical framework for the study of social narratives. In practice, however, an analysis need not necessarily rely on any one of these elements in isolation. Usually, a researcher adopts a more comprehensive framework by integrating more than one narrative element in the investigation, an approach that has some considerable advantages, as will be shown in what follows. The question, then, is not which element to study, but which element it would be heuristically advantageous to emphasize in a particular research project.

How would a researcher decide which element to emphasize in a particular narrative study? One way of addressing this dilemma is by probing the nature of the research question. For example, if a question specifically targets the narration strategy of an institution or the stories promoted by countries in conflict, the narrative element is embedded in the question itself.

To be sure, not every research question indicates explicitly whether the focus is on story, text, narration, or multiplicity. Yet, orienting a research project within the framework of these four narrative elements can be important in social narrative analysis. The analytic suggestions outlined as follows rest on a distinction between two levels of narrative analysis: "thin" and "thick" (Shenhav 2005b). In line with Clifford Geertz's well-known distinction between "thin" and "thick" descriptions (Geertz 1994: 213–31), these two analytical levels call for different research perspectives and emphasize different narrative elements.

A thin-level analysis is narrow in scope. In a previous study (Shenhav 2005b), I discussed the thin perspective, approaching it structurally as the "analysis of the organization of events in the narrative" (87). In this framework, the story figures as the main point of reference, with a limited textual element incorporated, mainly touching on the organization of events in the narrative (see later discussion). Theoretically, however, a narrow perspective can also involve both the text and the narration as major reference points—or even center on either of these elements alone. That said, a research project eliminating any reference to the story would, in my opinion, hardly constitute narrative analysis proper. As additional narrative elements are incorporated, which are related to the various strategies and means used by narrators to tell the story, analysis becomes thicker. Its scope and the analytic lens widen; the study is no longer concerned exclusively with the story, the text, or the narration, but with issues pertaining to all three.

Figure 7.1, in the shape of an inverted triangle, shows possible foci for social-narrative analysis in a sequence from thin to thick levels. The diagram provides a "road map" for orienting a narrative research project by bringing together both the thin–thick continuum and the narrative elements to be emphasized at its different points. The broken lines iconically represent the idea that the thin-thick distinction is not definitive or categorical, but rather is a matter of emphasis on certain elements in the accounts investigated, being largely subject to the researcher's discretion.

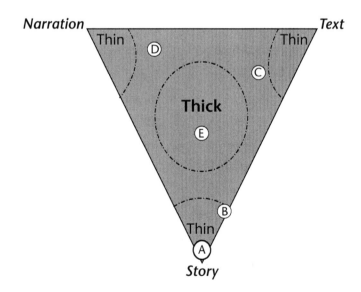

FIGURE 7.1 An analytical diagram for narrative research

Note: the broken lines demarcate the thin and thick levels of analysis. The letters A, B, C, D, and E mark the position of studies discussed in what follows.

The following sections describe in more detail the methodological implications of positioning a study on the thin–thick narrative-analytic continuum.

Thin-level narrative analysis. A scholar may find it helpful to start a social-narrative research project with a thin descriptive exegesis of the story alone, even if only as a preliminary stage. Some research projects may stay at the thin level (e.g., indicated by the letters A and B in Figure 7.1). Reconstructing the story is one possible option for conducting research at the thin level. A researcher may, for example, examine different narratives created on the same occasion. A simple way to proceed would be by writing down the events and characters for each narrative examined and arranging them in chronological order (see Figure 2.1 in Chapter 2). The resulting lists of events and characters make it possible to compare stories told by different narrators or in different circumstances.

One of the advantages of thin-level analysis is that it allows the study of a relatively large number of narratives. Various computer programs are available today that can facilitate such an examination (see review in Franzosi 2010), though to the best of my knowledge, there is no reliable automatic way to reconstruct stories from texts.

As discussed in Chapter 2, to identify the stories in narratives, a researcher may opt to code the texts, either using a simple table (see Table 2.1), or visually, with the help of a graphic representation such as the one demonstrated in Chapter 2 (see Figure 2.1).

Figure 7.1 indicates that a thin-level analysis is also possible from the textual and narrational perspectives—although, as previously mentioned, undertaking any narrative analysis without a substantive reference to the element of story appears problematic *a priori*. Still, one could perform a thin-level textual narrative analysis by, for example, counting words without consideration to the story. An example of a thin-level narrational analysis that does not take the story into account would be developing a typology of narrators, dissociated from their textual characterization. Most thin-level analyses, however, are likely to rest on the study of story.

Towards the center of the inverted triangle. Assuming that a social-narrative research project would typically begin with a thin-level analysis of the story, incorporating some textual and narrational aspects would move the researcher upwards, from the apex of the inverted triangle to augmented levels of analytic thickness.

Location B in Figure 7.1 marks a study at the edge of the thin area where a limited textual perspective receives attention. For example, comparing the order of events represented in the text to that in the story adds some textual elements to the analysis. The same applies if the analysis includes the number of times an event is mentioned in the text, which can be indicative, for instance, of intended emphasis (see the discussion on frequency in Chapter 3). Another way of adding a textual parameter while maintaining this position in the inverted triangle is shown in Figure 5.2, in which the horizontal axis represents the order of the text (marked in paragraph numbers) and the vertical axis represents the periods of time referenced in the text. Such visualization is especially helpful in dealing with multitemporal discourse, in which a single text may reference different historical periods (Shenhav 2005a).

The position indicated by the letter C in the inverted triangle in Figure 7.1 designates a study at intermediate "thickness" level—it tends towards being a textual analysis but still takes into consideration the elements of story and, to a greater extent, of narration. An example can be a study that compares differences in the points of view in crime stories told in court by lawyers, the accused, and judges. The primary focus would be on the textual aspect revealing the point of view. Yet, the researcher would also explore how these points of view serve the purpose of telling the story and would thus incorporate into the study some elements of narration and story.

Questions focused on the element of narration are positioned along the upper left-hand side of the inverted triangle (letter D in Figure 7.1). An example can be a study on the use of character-narrators as opposed to non-character narrators. Still, such a study is not expected to be centered solely on the element of narration: the D position indicates that the element of text would receive a greater secondary focus than that of story.

Thick-level narrative analysis. Research positioned around the center of the inverted triangle (letter E in Figure 7.1) would be "thick," in the sense that the analysis would take into serious consideration all three classical elements of narrative analysis—the story, the text, and the narration.

When social context is incorporated in the investigation, a range of options for a thick-level analysis expands further still. Contextual analysis at the thick level is likely to be more attuned to the relations between the text and its societal, historical, political, and cultural surroundings. Analysis of the narrative is not abandoned, but attention to extra-textual elements is introduced, as well as to the communicational aspects of speech.[2]

Performing narrative analysis at the "thick" level requires considerable effort and extensive training to explore the text from the three-pronged perspective of story, text, and narration, especially when also taking into account contextual factors. A researcher would likewise need to maintain an analytical focus and at the same time transport him- or herself into the three different "worlds" discussed above: the storyworld of the narrative studied; the context in which the story was created or is being told, or both; and the research task-governed scholarly universe.

Oriented Multiplicity

I have thus far demonstrated the potential of applying the approach diagrammed in Figure 7.1 to social-narrative analysis with reference to the story-text-narration triplet. The study of the dispersion of narratives in the social domain—their multiplicity—is not so much about the triangle's thin-thick dimension as about the connections among several such triangles. These triangles, in line with the fractal analogue, represent the different versions of a multiplied narrative, as Figure 7.2 illustrates. However, in a study of multiplicity, orienting a research project *within* the inverted triangle is still important as a means to clarify the focus of investigation.

An analysis of multiplicity can be carried out either at a thin level as indicated by the arrows at the corners of the inverted triangles, or at a thick level, as indicated by the arrow at their center (see Figure 7.2).

For example, as elucidated in Chapter 5, a structural approach to the study of multiplicity is projected to the lower, analytically thin sections of the inverted triangles in Figure 7.2, corresponding to the letter A or B in Figure 7.1, where the focus is on the story. A study centered either on the story or on the time-theme alone, to the exclusion of the text, would be positioned at the very bottom of the triangles in Figure 7.2. Alternatively, a study of multiplicity can be positioned at the thick level at the center of the inverted triangles. The latter option addresses the process of narrative reproduction, incorporating stories (possibly starting with the more basic unit of time-theme), texts, narration, and perhaps even contextual elements.

Studying a large number of narratives. A scholar may opt to study a number of narratives within the scope of a single research project. The reasons for such a decision could be many and varied, for example, focusing on multiplicity,

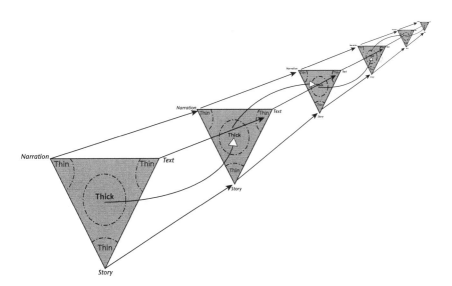

FIGURE 7.2 Analytical diagrams in the study of narrative multiplicity

Note: each inverted triangle stands for a different version of a narrative as it multiplies across time and/or space. The arrows represent the element(s) to be investigated and the analytical path the researcher intends to follow in examining narrative multiplicity.

rendering the sample more representative or more varied, exploring narrative changes, or carrying out comparative analyses.

An important *caveat* is in order at this point. It may prove challenging to conduct a thick-level analysis on a large number of narratives. In such a case, in consideration of research feasibility, it would be expedient to limit the number of narrative texts included in a study. There is no "gold standard" for the number of narratives that can be used in a research project. In some cases, an in-depth analysis of a single narrative can be telling enough, especially if that narrative is ubiquitous or powerful. Scholars who conduct a thick-level analysis, however, may want to study several narrative texts, either to compare among them or to validate the conclusions drawn from the study of one of the narratives.

Incorporating multiple narratives into a single study using a thick-level analysis can be accomplished in a variety of ways. One strategy to make the analysis of story, text, and narration in multiple narratives feasible could be to confine the investigation to selected segments of narrative texts. Such an analysis, while forfeiting the advantages inherent in exploring full narratives, can still be considered thick-level. (This is legitimate, as a single study cannot always be expected to cover every aspect of narrative complexity.) Another strategy would be to apply thick-level analysis to a single narrative and then corroborate the conclusions obtained based on other narratives. Yet another way to conduct a thick-level social-narrative analysis on several texts is by shifting back and forth among them. This strategy could be applied, for example, in a study of the political and societal role of narratives in Churchill's war speeches. This is not to say that the researcher would thereby avoid the labor-intensive phase of reading and interpreting each speech separately. Yet, this technique can help him or her meet the feasibility challenge of conducting thick-level narrative analysis based on several speeches.

Positioning your study. How might a researcher decide where in Figure 7.1 a research project should be positioned or where along the trajectory of multiple triangles in Figure 7.2 a narrative should be "pierced"? That choice would probably be informed by the question(s) he or she endeavors to address. Some questions lend themselves better to thick-level analysis, while others require a thinner level. A decision to this effect need not be made *a priori*; instead, a researcher may gravitate towards the needed focus during the course of a project. Whatever the case, the analytical diagrams (Figures. 7.1 and 7.2) introduced in this chapter can enhance a scholar's awareness of the various avenues available for conducting social-narrative analysis based on the narrative elements discussed in this book.

A Final Comment

Throughout this book I have examined various issues concerning the analysis and interpretation of social narratives, but I have said very little about those who actually perform the analysis. At the very beginning, I mentioned that the book's main objective is to improve the analytic story-listening skills of its readers. To this end, I discussed the concepts of narrative and social narrative, elaborated on three well-established narrative elements—story, text, and narration—and added a fourth one, multiplicity, which I believe to be crucial for understanding social narratives. In this final chapter, I have offered some guidelines for orienting research in relation to these four elements, with reference to thin vs. thick levels of analysis, and illustrated my analytic suggestions using the inverted triangle diagram.

Still, nowhere have I addressed the question of what makes one a good interpreter of narratives. The reason for this omission is simple: I don't know the answer. Surely, being familiar with theoretical frameworks, analytic methods, and other studies conducted in the field is a must; surely, being creative (Polkinghorne 2007) and sensitive to both implicit and explicit meanings of texts is a must. But this is not enough. My intuition tells me that good story-listeners may share something that makes them good story-interpreters as well, and thereby enables them to contribute, through their analytic and theoretical work, to the understanding of social narratives. Specifically, they all seem to share a tacit belief that, more often than not, one can find one's voice through listening to others. Maybe this should be the first thing to keep in mind when analyzing social narratives.

Notes

1. For an analysis of the interrelations between the researcher, his context, and the narrative see Polkinghorne (2007).
2. An extra-textual perspective was briefly elaborated previously, with reference to extra-textual narration in the discussion of narration (i.e., Chapter 4).

REFERENCES

Abbott, Porter H. 2008 [2002]. *The Cambridge Introduction to Narrative*. Cambridge: Cambridge University Press.
Alfeld, Peter. 1998. "Mandelbrot Set," *Understanding Mathematics*. University of Utah. http://www.math.utah.edu/~pa/math/mandelbrot/mandelbrot.html#algorithm (accessed September 18, 2014).
Andorra. 1921. *nationalanthems.info*. Edited by David Kendall. http://www.nationalanthems.info/ad.htm (accessed October 3, 2014).
Andrews, Molly. 2004. "Opening to the Original Contribution: Counter-Narratives and the Power to Oppose." In *Considering Counter Narratives: Narrating, Resisting, Making Sense*, edited by Michael Bamberg and Molly Andrews, 1–6. Amsterdam: John Benjamins.
Ankersmit, Frank. 2005. "Historiography." In *Routledge Encyclopedia of Narrative Theory*, edited by David Herman, Jahn Manfred, and Marie-Laure Ryan, 217–21. New York: Routledge.
Argyros, Alex. 1992. "Narrative and Chaos." *New Literary History* 23 (3): 659–73.
Aristotle. 2000. *The Poetics of Aristotle*, translated by S. H. Butcher, An Electronic Classics Series Publication. http://www2.hn.psu.edu/faculty/jmanis/aristotl/poetics.pdf (accessed January 28, 2015).
Aristotle. 2004. *Rhetoric*. Translated by W. R. Roberts. New York: Dover Publication.
Auerbach, Yehudith. 2009. "The Reconciliation Pyramid—A Narrative-Based Framework for Analyzing Identity Conflicts." *Political Psychology* 30 (2), 291–318.
Bakhtin, Mikhail M. 1981. *The Dialogic Imagination: Four Essays.* Translated by Caryl Emerson and Michael Holquist. Austin: University of Texas Press.
Bamberg, Michael. 2004. "Considering Counter Narratives." In *Considering Counter Narratives: Narrating, Resisting, Making Sense*, edited by Michael Bamberg and Molly Andrews, 351–71. Amsterdam: John Benjamins.
Bamberg, Michael. 2005. "Master Narrative." In *Routledge Encyclopedia of Narrative Theory*, edited by David Herman, Jahn Manfred, and Marie-Laure Ryan, 287–8. New York: Routledge.

References

Bamberg, Michael. 2006. "Introductory Remarks." *Narrative Inquiry* 16 (1): 1–2.

Baroni, Raphaël. 2011. "Tellability." In *The Living Handbook of Narratology*, edited by Peter Hühn et al. http://www.lhn.uni-hamburg.de/article/tellability (accessed November 15, 2013).

Bar-Tal, Daniel. 2000. *Shared Beliefs in a Society: Social Psychological Analysis*. Thousand Oaks, CA: Sage.

Bar-Tal, Daniel and Salomon, Gavriel. 2006. "Israeli-Jewish Narratives of the Israeli-Palestinian Conflict: Evolvement, Contents, Functions and Consequences." In *Israeli and Palestinian Narratives of Conflict: History's Double Helix*, edited by Robert I. Rotberg, 19–46. Bloomington: Indiana University Press.

Barthes, Roland. 1975 [1966]. "An Introduction to the Structural Analysis of Narrative." *New Literary History* 6 (2): 237–72.

Baudrillard, Jean. 1993. "After the Orgy." *The Transparency of Evil: Essays on Extreme Phenomena*. Translated by James Benedict, 3–31. London: Verso, 3–13.

Bazzanella, Carla. 2010. "Contextual Constraints in CMC Narratives." In *Narrative Revisited: Telling a Story in the Age of New Media*, edited by Christian R. Hoffmann, 19–37. Amsterdam: John Benjamins.

Benoit, William L. and Sheafer, Tamir. 2006. "Functional Theory and Political Discourse: Televised Debates in Israel and the United States." *Journalism & Mass Communication Quarterly* 83 (2): 281–97.

Bettelheim, Bruno. 1976. *The Uses of Enchantment: The Meaning and Importance of Fairy Tales*. New York: Knopf.

Bluck, Susan and Habermas, Tilmann. 2001. "Extending the Study of Autobiographical Memory: Thinking Back about Life across the Life Span." *Review of General Psychology* 5: 135–47.

Blum-Kulka, Shoshana. 1997. *Dinner Talk: Cultural Patterns of Sociability and Socialization in Family Discourse*. Mahwah, NJ: Lawrence Erlbaum.

Bonaparte, Napoleon. 2005 [1814]. "Farewell to the Old Guard", 20 April, 1814, in *Speeches that Changed the World*, edited by Simon S. Montefiore, 47. London: Quercus.

Borins, Sandford F. 2012. "Making Narrative Count: A Narratological Approach to Public Management Innovation." *Journal of Public Administration Research and Theory* 22 (1): 165–89.

Brummett, Barry. 2009. *Techniques of Close Reading*. Thousand Oaks, CA: Sage.

Bruner, Jerome. 1987. "Life as Narrative." *Social Research* 54 (1): 11–32.

Bush, George, W. 2001. "Inaugural Address." January 20, 2001. *The White House: Official Website of President George W. Bush*. http://whitehouse.georgewbush.org/news/2001/012001.asp (accessed September 20, 2014).

Calhoun, Craig. Ed. 2002. *Dictionary of the Social Sciences*. New York: Oxford University Press.

Carlisle, Janice. 1994. "Introduction." In *Narrative and Culture*, edited by Janice Carlisle and Daniel R. Schwarz, 1–12. Athens: University of Georgia Press.

Carr, David. 1986. "Narrative and the Real World: An Argument for Continuity." *History and Theory* 25 (2): 117–31.

Carrithers, Michael. 1991. "Narrativity: Mindreading and Making Societies." In *Natural Theories of Mind: Evolution, Development and Simulation of Everyday Mindreading*, edited by Andrew Whiten, 305–18. Oxford: Basil Blackwell.

Chase, Suzan E. 2008. "Narrative Inquiry: Multiple Lenses, Approaches, Voices." In *Collecting and Interpreting Qualitative Materials*, edited by Norman K. Denzin and Yvonna S. Lincoln, 57–94. Los Angeles: Sage.

Chatman, Seymour B. 1978. *Story and Discourse: Narrative Structure in Fiction and Film.* Ithaca, NY: Cornell University Press.

Churchill, Winston. 1941. "Joint Session of Congress, Washington 26 December, 1941." In *The Speeches of Winston Churchill*, edited by David Cannadine, 226–33. London: Penguin Books.

Clandinin, D. Jean and Rosiek, Jerry. 2007. "Mapping a Landscape of Narrative Inquiry: Borderland Spaces and Tensions." In *Handbook of Narrative Inquiry: Mapping a Methodology*, edited by D. Jean Clandinin, 35–75. London: Sage.

Clayman, Steven E. 1992. "Footing in the Achievement of Neutrality: The Case of News Interview Discourse." In *Talk at Work: Interaction in Institutional Settings*, edited by Drew Paul and John Heritage, 163–98. Cambridge: Cambridge University Press.

The Constitution of South Africa. 1996. http://www.gov.za/documents/constitution/1996/a108-96.pdf (accessed July 30, 2014).

Cornog, Evan. 2004. *The Power and the Story: How the Crafted Presidential Narrative Has Determined Political Success from George Washington to George W. Bush.* New York: Penguin Press.

Corsaro, William A. and Heise, David. 1990. "Event Structure Models from Ethnographic Data." *Sociological Methodology* 20 (1): 1–57.

Coste, Didier. 1989. *Narrative as Communication.* Minneapolis: University of Minnesota Press.

Czarniawska, Barbara. 2004. *Narratives in Social Science Research.* London: Sage.

Czarniawska, Barbara. 2010. "The Uses of Narratology in Social and Policy Studies." *Critical Policy Studies* 4 (1): 58–76.

Dannenberg, Hilary P. 2005a. "Plot." In *Routledge Encyclopedia of Narrative Theory*, edited by David Herman, Jahn Manfred, and Marie-Laure Ryan, 435–9. New York: Routledge.

Dannenberg, Hilary P. 2005b. "Plot Types." In *Routledge Encyclopedia of Narrative Theory*, edited by David Herman, Jahn Manfred, and Marie-Laure Ryan, 439–40. New York: Routledge.

Dershowitz, Alan M. 1996. "Life is Not a Dramatic Narrative." In *Law's Stories: Narrative and Rhetoric in the Law*, edited by Peter Brooks and Paul D. Gewirtz, 99–105. New Haven, CT: Yale University Press.

Devine-Wright, Patrick. 2003. "A Theoretical Overview of Memory and Conflict." In *The Role of Memory in Ethnic Conflict*, edited by Ed Cairns and Micheal D. Roe, 9–34. New York: Palgrave Macmillan.

Durham, Frank D. 1998. "News frames as social narratives: TWA Flight 800." *Journal of Communication*, 48(4): 100–17.

Eggins, Suzanne and Slade, Diana. 1997. *Analyzing Casual Conversation.* London: Cassell.

Elliott, Jane. 2005. *Using Narrative in Social Research: Qualitative and Quantitative Approaches.* London: Sage.

Entman, Robert M. 2008. "Theorizing Mediated Public Diplomacy: The U.S. Case." *International Journal of Press/Politics* 13: 87–102.

Ezrahi, Yaron. 2012. *Imagined Democracies: Necessary Political Fictions.* Cambridge: Cambridge University Press.

Fischer, Frank. 2003. *Reframing Public Policy: Discursive Politics and Deliberative Practices.* New York: Oxford University Press.

Fisher, Walter R. 1985. "The Narrative Paradigm: an Elaboration." *Communication Monographs* 52: 347–67.

Fludernik, Monika. 1996. *Towards a "Natural" Narratology.* New York: Routledge.

Fludernik, Monika. 2009. *An Introduction to Narratology*. New York: Routledge.
Forster, Edward M. 1927. *Aspects of the Novel*. New York: Harcourt Brace.
Foss, Sonja K. 2009. *Rhetorical Criticism*, 4th edition. Long Grove: Waveland Press.
Frank, Arthur W. 2010. *Letting Stories Breathe: A Socio-Narratology*. Chicago: University of Chicago Press.
Frank, Arthur W. 2013 [1995]. *The Wounded Storyteller: Body, Illness, and Ethics*. Chicago: University of Chicago Press.
Franzosi, Roberto. 1998. "Narrative Analysis—Or Why (And How) Sociologists Should Be Interested in Narrative." *Annual Review of Sociology* 24: 517–54.
Franzosi, Roberto. 2004. *From Words to Numbers: Narrative, Data and Social Science*. New York: Cambridge University Press.
Franzosi, Roberto. 2010. *Quantitative Narrative Analysis*. Los Angeles: Sage.
Gane, Mike. 2000. *Jean Baudrillard: In Radical Uncertainty*. London: Pluto Press.
Geertz, Clifford. 1994. "Thick Description: Toward an Interpretive Theory of Culture." In *Reading in the Philosophy of Social Science*, edited by Michael Martin and Lee C. McIntyre, 213–31. Cambridge, MA: MIT Press.
Genette, Gérard. 1980 [1972]. *Narrative Discourse*. Translated by Jane E. Lewin. Ithaca, NY: Cornell University Press.
George VI. 1939a. "Outbreak of War with Germany, 3 September 1939." *Historical Royal Speeches and Writings*. The British Monarchy website. http://www.royal.gov.uk/pdf/georgevi.pdf (accessed December 21, 2013).
George VI. 1939b. "Christmas Day Broadcast, 1939." *Historical Royal Speeches and Writings*. The British Monarchy website. http://www.royal.gov.uk/pdf/georgevi.pdf (accessed December 21, 2013).
Global Language Monitor. 2010. Top Words. http://www.languagemonitor.com/category/words-of-the-decade/ (accessed November 30, 2013).
Goddard, Jay A., Lehr, Ron, and Lapadat, Judith C. 2000. "Parents of Children with Disabilities: Telling a Different Story." *Canadian Journal of Counseling* 34: 273–89.
Goffman, Erving. 1981. *Forms of Talk*. Philadelphia: University of Pennsylvania Press.
Green, Melanie C. 2008. "Transportation Theory." In *The International Encyclopedia of Communication*, edited by Wolfgang Donsbach. Malden, MA: Wiley/Blackwell (Blackwell Reference Online, accessed March 7, 2010).
Green, Melanie C. and Brock, Timothy C. 2000. "The Role of Transportation in the Persuasiveness of Public Narratives." *Journal of Personality and Social Psychology* 79 (5): 701–21.
Griffin, Larry J. 1993. "Narrative, Event-Structure Analysis and Causal Interpretation in Historical Sociology." *American Journal of Sociology* 98 (5): 1094–1133.
Grube, Dennis. 2012. "Prime Ministers and Political Narratives for Policy Change: Towards a Heuristic." *Policy & Politics* 40 (4): 569–86.
Gubrium, Jaber F. and Holstein, James A. 2009. *Analyzing Narrative Reality*. Thousand Oaks, CA: Sage.
Hajer, Maarten A. 1995. *The Politics of Environmental Discourse: Ecological Modernization and the Policy Process*. Oxford: Oxford University Press.
Hammack, Phillip L. and Pilecki, Andrew. 2012. "Narrative as a Root Metaphor for Political Psychology." *Political Psychology* 33 (1): 75–103.
Heinen, Sandra and Sommer, Roy. 2009. "Narratology and Interdisciplinarity." In *Narratology in the Age of Cross-Disciplinary Narrative Research*, Vol. 20, edited by Sandra Heinen and Roy Sommer, 1–10. Berlin: Walter de Gruyter.
Heise, David R. 1991. "Event Structure Analysis: A Qualitative Model of Quantitative Research." In *Using Computers in Qualitative Research*, edited by Nigel G. Fielding and Raymond Lee, 136–63. Newbury Park, CA: Sage.

Heise, David R. 2014. *Event Structure Analysis*. David R. Heise's World Wide Web site at Indiana University, Bloomington, http://www.indiana.edu/~socpsy/ESA/Ethno Help.pdf (accessed February 19, 2014).
Herman, David. 1999. "Toward a Socionarratology: New Ways of Analyzing Natural-language Narratives." In *Narratologies: New Perspectives on Narrative Analysis*, edited by David Herman, 218–46. Columbus: Ohio State University Press.
Herman, David. 2002. *Story Logic: Problems and Possibilities of Narrative*. Lincoln: University of Nebraska Press.
Herman, David. 2005a. "Fabula." In *Routledge Encyclopedia of Narrative Theory*, edited by David Herman, Jahn Manfred, and Marie-Laure Ryan, 157. New York: Routledge.
Herman, David. 2005b. "Sjuzhet." In *Routledge Encyclopedia of Narrative Theory*, edited by David Herman, Jahn Manfred, and Marie-Laure Ryan, 535. New York: Routledge.
Herman, David. 2005c. "Schemata." In *Routledge Encyclopedia of Narrative Theory*, edited by David Herman, Jahn Manfred, and Marie-Laure Ryan, 513–14. New York: Routledge.
Herman, David. 2009. *Basic Elements of Narrative*. Malden, MA: Wiley-Blackwell.
Herman, David. 2012. "Exploring the Nexus of Narrative and Mind." In *Narrative Theory: Core Concepts and Critical Debates*, edited by David Herman, James Phelan, Peter J. Rabinowitz, Brian Richardson, and Robyn Warhol, 14–19. Columbus: Ohio State University Press.
Herman, David, Manfred, Jahn, and Ryan, Marie-Laure. 2005a. "Analepsis." In *Routledge Encyclopedia of Narrative Theory*, edited by David Herman, Jahn Manfred, and Marie-Laure Ryan, 14. New York: Routledge.
Herman, David, Manfred, Jahn, and Ryan, Marie-Laure. 2005b. "Prolepsis." In *Routledge Encyclopedia of Narrative Theory*, edited by David Herman, Jahn Manfred, and Marie-Laure Ryan, 468. New York: Routledge.
Herman, David, Manfred, Jahn, and Ryan, Marie-Laure. Eds. 2005c. *Routledge Encyclopedia of Narrative Theory*. New York: Routledge.
Herman, Luc and Vervaeck, Bart. 2005. *Handbook of Narrative Analysis*. Lincoln: University of Nebraska Press.
Holsti, Ole R. 1969. *Content Analysis for the Social Sciences and Humanities*. Reading, MA: Addison-Wesley.
Hyvärinen, Matti. 2006. "An Introduction to Narrative Travels." *Collegium* 1: 3–9.
Ireland, Ken. 2005. "Temporal Ordering." In *Routledge Encyclopedia of Narrative Theory*, edited by David Herman, Jahn Manfred, and Marie-Laure Ryan, 591–2. New York: Routledge.
Iser, Wolfgang. 1974. *The Implied. Reader. Patterns of Communication in Prose Fiction from Bunyan to Beckett*. Baltimore: Johns Hopkins University Press.
Ish-Shalom, Piki. 2013. "Nonkilling Society as a Lighthouse Narrative." In *Nonkilling Security and the State*, edited by Joám Evans Pim 69–83. Honolulu, HI and Omaha, NE: Center for Global Nonkilling and Creighton University.
Jannidis, Fotis. 2012. "Character." In *The Living Handbook of Narratology*, edited by Peter Hühn et al. Hamburg: Hamburg University Press. http://www.lhn.uni-hamburg.de/article/character (accessed November 15, 2013).
Jaworski, Adam and Coupland, Nikolas. Eds. 1999. *The Discourse Reader*. New York: Routledge.
Jefferson, Thomas. 1801. "Inaugural Address," March 4, 1801. Online by Gerhard Peters and John T. Woolley, *The American Presidency Project*. http://www.presidency.ucsb.edu/ws/?pid=25803 (accessed June 31, 2014).
Johnson, Lyndon B. 1965. "The President's Address at Johns Hopkins University: Peace without Conquest." *Public Papers of the Presidents of the United States: Lyndon B.*

Johnson, 1965. Vol. 1, entry 172, pp. 394–9. Washington, DC: Government Printing Office. See also http://www.lbjlibrary.org/exhibits/the-presidents-address-at-johns-hopkins-university-peace-without-conquest (accessed December 3, 2013).

Jones, Michael D., and McBeth, Mark K. 2010. "A Narrative Policy Framework: Clear Enough to Be Wrong?" *Policy Studies Journal* 38(2), 329–53.

Jovchelovitch, Sandra and Bauer, Martin W. 2000. "Narrative Interviewing." In *Qualitative Researching with Text, Image and Sound*, edited by Martin W. Bauer and George Gaskell, 57–74. London: Sage.

King, Martin L. 1963. "Speech by the Rev. Martin Luther King at the 'March on Washington.'" http://www.archives.gov/press/exhibits/dream-speech.pdf (accessed September 10, 2014).

Koren-Karie, Nina, Oppenheim, David, and Getzler-Yosef, Rachel. 2008. "Shaping Children's Internal Working Models Through Mother–Child Dialogues: The Importance of Resolving Past Maternal Trauma." *Attachment & Human Development* 10 (4): 465–83.

Kosenko, Kami and Laboy, Johanne. 2013. "'I Survived': The Content and Forms of Survival Narratives." *Journal of Loss and Trauma*, online first. DOI:10.1080/15325024.2013.808948

Krebs, Ronald R. Forthcoming a. *Narrative and the Making of U.S. National Security*. Cambridge: Cambridge University Press.

Krebs, Ronald R. Forthcoming b. "How Dominant Narratives Rise and Fall: Military Conflict, Politics, and the Cold War Consensus." *International Organization*.

Krebs, Ronald R. and Lobasz, Jennifer K. 2007. "Fixing the Meaning of 9/11: Hegemony, Coercion, and the Road to War in Iraq." *Security Studies* 16 (3): 409–51.

Kristeva, Julia. 1970. *Le Texte du Roman: Approche Sémiologique d'une Structure Discursive*. The Hague: Mouton.

Kroeber, Karl. 1992. *Retelling/Rereading: The Fate of Storytelling in Modern Times*. New Brunswick, NJ: Rutgers University Press.

Kukkonen, Karin. 2014. "Plot." In *The Living Handbook of Narratology*, edited by Peter Hühn et al. http://www.lhn.uni-hamburg.de/article/plot (accessed February 19, 2014).

Labov, William. 1972. *Language in the Inner City: Studies in the Black English Vernacular*. Philadelphia: University of Pennsylvania Press.

Labov, William. 1997. "Some Further Steps in Narrative Analysis." *Journal of Narrative and Life History* 7: 395–415.

Labov, William and Waletzky, Joshua. 1967. "Narrative Analysis: Oral Versions of Personal Experience." In *Essays on the Verbal and Visual Arts: Proceedings of the American Ethnological Society*, edited by June Helm, 12–44. Seattle: American Ethnological Society.

Lacretelle, C. 1829. *Histoire de France, depuis la Restauration*, Vol. 1. Paris: Delaunay (in French).

Lejano, Raul P. and Leong, Ching. 2012. "A Hermeneutic Approach to Explaining and Understanding Public Controversies." *Journal of Public Administration Research and Theory* 22 (4): 793–814.

Levinson, Stephen C. 1988. "Putting Linguistics on a Proper Footing: Explorations in Goffman's Concepts of Participation." In: *Erving Goffman: Exploring the Interaction Order*, edited by Paul Drew and Anthony Wootton, 161–227. Cambridge: Polity Press.

Linde, Charlotte. 1993. *Life Stories: The Creation of Coherence*. New York: Oxford University Press.

Linde, Charlotte. 2009. *Working the Past: Narrative and Institutional Memory*. New York: Oxford University Press.

Lyotard, Jean-Francois. 1984. *The Postmodern Condition*. Manchester: Manchester University Press.

MacIntyre, Alasdair. 1981. *After Virtue: A Study in Moral Theory*. Notre Dame: University of Notre Dame Press.

MacKinnon, Catharine A. 1996. "Law's Stories as Reality and Politics." in *Law's Stories. New Haven*, edited by P. Brooks and P. Gewirtz. 232–8. New Haven, CT: Yale University Press.

Mandelbrot, Benoit B. 1977. *Fractals: Form, Chance, and Dimension*. San Francisco: W. H. Freeman.

Maynard-Moody, Steven and Musheno, Michael. 2006. "Stories for Research." In *Interpretation and Method: Empirical Research Methods and the Interpretive Turn*, edited by Dvora Yanow and Peregrine Schwartz-Shea, 316–30. Armonk, NY: M. E. Sharp.

McAdams, Dan P. 2001. "The Psychology of Life Stories." *Review of General Psychology* 5 (2): 100–22.

Miller, J. Hillis. 2005. "Henry James and 'Focalization' or Why James Loves Gyp." In *A Companion to Narrative Theory*, edited by James Phelan and Peter J. Rabinowitz, 124–35. Oxford: Blackwell.

Milner, Ryan M. 2013. "Pop Polyvocality: Internet Memes, Public Participation, and the Occupy Wall Street Movement." *International Journal of Communication*, 7 (34), 2357–90.

Mink, Louis O. 1987. "Narrative Form as a Cognitive Instrument." In: *Historical Understanding*, edited by Brian Fay, Eugene O. Golob, and Richard T. Vann, 183–99. Ithaca, NY: Cornell University Press.

Mishler, Elliot G. 1986. *Research Interviewing: Context and Narrative*. Cambridge, MA: Harvard University Press.

Mishler, Elliot G. 1995. "Models of Narrative Analysis: A Typology." *Journal of Narrative and Life History* 5 (2): 87–123.

Mitrani, Mor. 2013. "(Re-)telling Societal Beliefs: Changing Narratives in Israel's Political Discourse Regarding Transition to Peace." *International Journal of Conflict Management*, 24 (3): 245–64.

Moraru, Christian. 2005. "Intertextuality." In *Routledge Encyclopedia of Narrative Theory*, edited by David Herman, Jahn Manfred, and Marie-Laure Ryan, 256–61. New York: Routledge.

National Coalition of Tea Party Affiliates. 2013. "Voice of the Tea Party Movement." http://www.teaparty-usa.com/Tea_Party.html (accessed December 11, 2013).

Nelson, Katherine. 2003. "Self and Social Functions: Individual Autobiographical Memory and Collective Narrative." *Memory* 11 (2): 125–36.

Nelson, Katherine. 2004. "Construction of the Cultural Self in Early Narratives." In *Narrative Analysis: Studying the Development of Individuals in Society*, edited by Colette Daiute and Cynthia Lightfoot, 87–109. Thousand Oaks, CA: Sage.

Neuman, W. Russell, Just, Marion R., and Crigler, Ann N. 1992. *Common Knowledge: News and the Construction of Political Meaning*. Chicago: University of Chicago Press.

Norquay, Naomi. 1999. "Identity and Forgetting." *Oral History Review* 26 (1): 1–21.

Nünning, Ansgar. 2005. "Implied Author." In *Routledge Encyclopedia of Narrative Theory*, edited by David Herman, Jahn Manfred, and Marie-Laure Ryan, 239–40. New York: Routledge.

Obama, Barack. 2008. "US Election: Full Text of Barack Obama's Speech on the Economy," *The Guardian*, http://www.theguardian.com/world/2008/oct/13/uselections2008-barackobama (accessed November 15, 2013).

References

Ochs, Elinor. 1997. "Narrative." In *Discourse as Structure and Process*, Vol. 1, edited by Teun A. van Dijk, 185–207. London: Sage.

Oxford English Dictionary Online Edition. s.v. "fractal." http://www.oed.com/view/Entry/74094?redirectedFrom=fractal#eid (accessed January 29, 2015).

Oxford English Dictionary Online Edition. s.v. "text." http://www.oed.com/view/Entry/200002?rskey=CAMdux&result=1&isAdvanced=false#eid (accessed December 5, 2013).

Palin, Sarah. 2011. Governor Palin's Speech at the "Restoring America" Tea Party of America Rally in Indianola, Iowa" (Video and Transcript). http://sarahpac.com/posts/governor-palins-speech-at-the-restoring-america-tea-party-of-america-rally-in-indianola-iowa-video-and-transcript (accessed July 30, 2014).

Patterson, Molly and Monroe, Kristen. R. 1998. "Narrative in Political Science," *Annual Review of Political Science*, 1: 315–331.

Phelan, James and Booth, Wayne C. 2005. "Narrator." In *Routledge Encyclopedia of Narrative Theory*, edited by David Herman, Jahn Manfred, and Marie-Laure Ryan, 388–92. New York: Routledge.

Polkinghorne, Donald. E. 1988. *Narrative Knowing and the Human Sciences*. New York: State University of New York Press.

Polkinghorne, Donald E. 2007. "Validity Issues in Narrative Research," *Qualitative Inquiry* 13 (4): 471–86.

Polletta, Francesca, Chen, Pang C. B., Gardner, Beth G., and Motes, Alice. 2011. "The Sociology of Storytelling." *Annual Review of Sociology* 37: 109–30.

Ponti, Marisa. 2012. "Uncovering Causality in Narratives of Collaboration: Actor-Network Theory and Event Structure Analysis." *Forum Qualitative Sozialforschung/Forum: Qualitative Social Research* 13 (1). http://www.qualitative-research.net/index.php/fqs/article/view/1659/3281

Propp, Vladimir I. 1968 [1927]. *Morphology of the Folk Tale*, Vol. 9. Austin: University of Texas Press.

Renan, Ernest. 1990 [1882]. "What is a Nation?" In *Nation and Narration*, edited by H. K. Bhabha, 8–22. London: Routledge.

Ricoeur, Paul. 1980. "Narrative Time." *Critical Inquiry* 7 (1): 169–90.

Ricoeur, Paul. 1984. *Time and Narrative (Temps et Récit)*, Vol. 1. Translated by Kathleen McLaughlin and David Pellauer. Chicago: University of Chicago Press.

Ricoeur, Paul. 1991. "Narrative Identity." Translated by Mark S. Muldoon. *Philosophy Today* 35: 73–81.

Riessman, Catherine K. Ed. 1993. *Narrative Analysis*, Vol. 30. Newbury Park, CA: Sage.

Riessman, Catherine K. 2008. *Narrative Methods for the Human Sciences*. Los Angeles: Sage.

Rimmon-Kenan, Shlomith. 2002 [1983]. *Narrative Fiction: Contemporary Poetics*, 2nd edition. London: Routledge.

Rimmon-Kenan, Shlomith. 2006. "Concepts of Narrative." *Collegium* 1: 10–19.

Romanowska-Pawliczek, Anna, Pawliczek, Piotr, and Sołtys, Zbigniew. 2009. "Algorithm for Treelike Structures Generation" in *Computers in Medical Activity*, Vol. 65, edited by Edward Kacki, Marek Rudnicki, and Joanna Stempczynska, 255–63. Berlin: Springer.

Rorty, Richard. 1998. *Achieving Our Country: Leftist Thought in Twentieth-Century America*. Cambridge, MA: Harvard University Press.

Ryan, Marie-Laure. 2005. "On the Theoretical Foundations of Transmedial Narratology." In *Narratology beyond Literary Criticism: Mediality, Disciplinarity*, edited by Jan Christoph Meister, 1–24. Berlin: Walter de Gruyter.

Saleebey, Dennis. 1994. "Culture, Theory, and Narrative: The Intersection of Meanings in Practice." *Social Work* 39 (4): 351–9.

Salomon, Gavriel and Biton, Yifat. 2006. "Peace in the Eyes of Israeli and Palestinian Youths: Effects of Collective Narratives and Peace Education Program." *Journal of Peace Research* 43 (2): 167–80.

Sarbin, Theodore R. 2004. "The Role of Imagination in Narrative Construction." In *Narrative Analysis: Studying the Development of Individuals in Society*, edited by Colette Daiute and Cynthia Lightfoot, 5–20. Thousand Oaks, CA: Sage.

Schmid, Wolf. 2010. *Narratology: An Introduction*. New York: Walter de Gruyter.

Schwartz-Shea, Peregrine. 2002. "Theorizing Gender for Experimental Game Theory: Experiments with 'Sex Status' and 'Merit Status' in an Asymmetric Game." *Sex Roles* 47 (7–8): 301–19.

Scott, James C. 1990. *Domination and the Arts of Resistance: Hidden Transcripts*. New Haven, CT: Yale University Press.

Seidler, David. 2010. *The King's Speech*. Directed by Tom Hooper. Produced by Iain Canning, Emile Sherman, and Gareth Unwin. London: The Weinstein Company and UK Film Council in association with Momentum Pictures.

Shanahan, Elizabeth A., Jones, Michael D., and McBeth, Mark K. 2011. "Policy Narratives and Policy Processes." *Policy Studies Journal* 39 (3): 535–61.

Sheafer, Tamir and Shenhav, Shaul R. 2009. "Mediated Public Diplomacy in a New Era of Warfare." *Communication Review* 12 (3): 272–83.

Sheafer, Tamir, Shenhav, Shaul R., and Goldstein, Kenneth. 2011. "Voting for Our Story: A Narrative Model of Electoral Choice in Multiparty Systems." *Comparative Political Studies* 44 (3): 313–38.

Shearing, Clifford D. and Ericson, Richard V. 1991. "Culture as Figurative Action." *British Journal of Sociology* 42 (4): 481–506.

Shen, Dan. 2002. "Defense and Challenge: Reflections on the Relation between Story and Discourse." *Narrative* 10 (3): 222–43.

Shenhav, Shaul R. 2005a. "Concise Narratives: A Structural Analysis of Political Discourse." *Discourse Studies* 7: 313–35.

Shenhav, Shaul R. 2005b. "Thin and Thick Narrative Analysis: On the Question of Defining and Analyzing Political Narratives." *Narrative Inquiry* 15 (1): 75–99.

Shenhav, Shaul R. 2006. "Political Narratives and Political Reality." *International Political Science Review* 27: 245–62.

Shenhav, Shaul R. 2009. "We Have a Place in a Long Story: Empowered Narratives and the Construction of Communities: The Case of US Presidential Debates." *Narrative Inquiry* 19 (2): 199–218.

Shenhav, Shaul R., Oshri, Odelia, Ofek, Dganit, and Sheafer, Tamir. 2014. "Story Coalitions: Applying Narrative Theory to the Study of Coalition Formation." *Political Psychology* 35 (5): 661–78.

Shenhav, Shaul R., Sheafer, Tamir, and Gabay, Itay. 2010. "Incoherent Narrator: Israeli Public Diplomacy During the Disengagement and the Elections in the Palestinian Authority." *Israel Studies* 15 (3): 143–62.

Shifman, Limor. 2013. *Memes in Digital Culture*. Cambridge, MA: MIT Press.

Singer, Jefferson A. 2004. "Narrative Identity and Meaning Making across the Adult Lifespan: An Introduction." *Journal of Personality* 72 (3): 437–59.

Somers, Margaret R. 1994. "The Narrative Constitution of Identity: A Relational and Network Approach." *Theory and Society* 23: 605–49.

Somers, Margaret R. and Gibson, Gloria D. 1994. "Reclaiming the Epistemological 'Other': Narrative and the Social Constitution of Identity." In *Social Theory and the Politics of Identity*, edited by Craig Calhoun, 37–99. Oxford: Blackwell.

Sparks, Holloway. 1997. "Dissident Citizenship: Democratic Theory, Political Courage, and Activist Women." *Hypatia* 12(4): 74–110.
Squire, Corinne, Andrews, Molly, and Tamboukou, Maria. 2013. "Introduction: What is Narrative Research." In *Doing Narrative Research*, 2nd edition, edited by Molly Andrews, Corinne Squire, and Maria Tamboukou, 1–26. Los Angeles: Sage.
St. Clair, William. 2004. *The Reading Nation in the Romantic Period*. Cambridge: Cambridge University Press.
Steinmetz, George. 1992. "Reflections on the Role of Social Narratives in Working-Class Formation: Narrative Theory in the Social Sciences." *Social Science History* 16 (3): 489–516.
Stone, Deborah. 1989. "Causal Stories and the Formation of Policy Agendas." *Political Science Quarterly* 104 (2): 281–300.
Suny, Ronald G. 1998. *The Soviet Experiment*. New York: Oxford University Press.
Tannen, Deborah. 2008. " 'We've Never Been Close, We're Very Different': Three Narrative Types in Sister Discourse." *Narrative Inquiry* 18 (2): 206–29.
Taylor, Charles. 1971. "Interpretation and the sciences of man." *Review of Metaphysics*, 25 (1), 3–51.
The State of Israel. 1948. "The Declaration of the Establishment of the State of Israel." Israel Minister of Foreign Affairs. http://www.mfa.gov.il/mfa/foreignpolicy/peace/guide/pages/declaration%20of%20establishment%20of%20state%20of%20israel.aspx
The Times. 1939. "A Copy for Every Household." September 4, 1939: 5.
Todorov, Tzvetan. 1966. "Les catégories du récit littéraire." *Communications* 8: 125–51.
Toolan, Michael J. 2001. *Narrative: A Critical Linguistic Introduction*. New York: Routledge.
van Dijk, Teun A. 1993a. "Stories and Racism." In *Narrative and Social Control*, edited by Dennis K. Mumby, 121–42. Newbury Park: Sage.
van Dijk, Teun A. 1993b. "Principles of Critical Discourse Analysis." *Discourse & Society* 4 (2): 249–83.
van Eeten, Michel J. G. 2007. "Narrative Policy Analysis." In *Handbook of Public Policy Analysis: Theory, Politics and Methods*, No.3, edited by Frank Fischer, Gerald J. Miller, and Mara S. Sidney, 251–69. Boca Raton, FL: CRC Press.
van Hulst, Merlijn. 2013. "Storytelling at the Police Station: The Canteen Culture Revisited." *British Journal of Criminology* 53 (4): 624–42.
Vinitzky-Seroussi, Vered. 2001. "Commemorating Narratives of Violence: The Yitzhak Rabin Memorial Day in Israeli Schools." *Qualitative Sociology* 24 (2): 245–68.
Wade, Alex. 2014. "Social Metaphors and Meaning in Fourth Order Simulacra." *International Journal of Baudrillard Studies* 11 (1).
Waitzkin, Howard and Magana, Holly. 1997. "The Black Box in Somatization: Unexplained Physical Symptoms, Culture, and Narratives of Trauma." *Social Science & Medicine* 45 (6): 811–25.
Wallin, Hans. 1989. "Interpolating and Orthogonal Polynomials on Fractals." *Constructive Approximation* 5(1), 137–50.
Wasik, Bill. 2009. *And Then There's This: How Stories Live and Die in Viral Culture*. New York: Penguin.
Weber, Max. 1949 [1905]. *The Methodology of the Social Sciences*. New York: Free Press.
White, Hayden. 1975. *Metahistory: The Historical Imagination in Nineteenth-Century Europe*. Baltimore: Johns Hopkins University Press.
White, Hayden. 1980. "The Value of Narrativity in the Representation of Reality." *Critical Inquiry* 7 (1), 5–27.
Whitebrook, Maureen. 2001. *Identity, Narrative and Politics*. London: Routledge.

Widdershoven, Guy A. 1993. "The Story of Life: Hermeneutic Perspectives on the Relationship between Narrative and Life History." In *The Narrative Study of Lives*, Vol. 1, edited by Ruthellen Josselson and Amia Lieblich, 1–20. London: Sage.

World Health Organization. 2007. *Working for Health: An Introduction to the World Health Organization*. Geneva: WHO Press. http://www.who.int/about/brochure_en.pdf (accessed December 5, 2013).

Yanow, Dvora. 1995. "Built Space as Story: The Policy Stories That Buildings Tell." *Policy Studies Journal* 23 (3): 407–22.

Yanow, Dvora. 1996. *How Does a Policy Mean?: Interpreting Policy and Organizational Actions*. Washington, DC: Georgetown University Press.

Yanow, Dvora. 2007. "Qualitative-Interpretive Methods in Policy Research." In *The Handbook of Public Policy Analysis: Theory, Politics and Methods*, edited by Frank Fischer, Gerald J. Miller, and Mara S. Sidney, 405–15. Boca Raton, FL: CRC Press.

Yanow, Dvora. 2014. "Thinking Interpretively: Philosophical Presuppositions and the Human Sciences." In *Interpretation and Method: Empirical Research Methods and the Interpretive Turn*, 2nd edition, 5–26. New York: M. E. Sharpe.

Yevseyev, Vyacheslav. 2005. "Measuring Narrativity in Literary Text." In *Narratology beyond Literary Criticism*, edited by Jan Christoph Meister in collaboration with Tom Kindth and Wilhelm Schernus, 109–24. Berlin: Walter de Gruyter.

Young, James E. 1993. *The Texture of Memory: Holocaust Memorials and Meaning*. New Haven, CT: Yale University Press.

Zerubavel, Yael. 1995. *Recovered Roots: Collective Memory and the Making of Israeli National Tradition*. Chicago: University of Chicago Press.

Zilber, Tamar B. 2009. "Institutional Maintenance as Narrative Acts." In *Institutional Work*, edited by Thomas B. Lawrence, Roy Suddaby, and Bernard Leca, 205–35. Cambridge: Cambridge University Press.

Zipes, Jack David. 1994. *Fairy Tale as Myth/Myth as Fairy Tale*. Lexington: University Press of Kentucky.

INDEX

Page numbers in *italics* indicate figures or tables.

Alfeld, Peter 60, *61*, 68n3
Andorra (national anthem) 80–1
animators 49, *53*, 74–5
Argyros, Alexander 60
Aristotle 9, 14, 26, 55n2
audience 52–3, 76–7
authors 49, 51–2, *53*

Barthes, Roland 2, 9
Benoit, William L. 27
Bonaparte, Napoleon 26–7
Bruner, Jerome 72
Bush, George W. 4

Carr, David 70
catalysts 32, *34*
causality 13, 29–31
causal stories 30
character narrators 50, 51, *53*
characters in the social domain 25–7
Churchill, Winston 4–5, 40–2, 51–2, 53, 76, 86
closure 4–5, 14, 36
coding texts 27, *28*
coherence 13
collective narratives, as term 17
competing stories 78
complication-resolution plot type 33–4
concise narratives 62–5, *63*, *66*
context-time 42–3, *45*

core elements 59–60, 62–5, *63*, *66*
Coste, Didier 15
counterfactual relations 31–2
critical discourse analysis 53, 78

Declaration of the Establishment of the State of Israel *63*, 63–5
Dershowitz, Alan 72
discourse 5, 11–16, 21–5, 27, 35, 42, 74–5, 78, 84
discourse analysis 5, 12, 74
dominant stories 75, 77–8
duration 43–4, *45*

economic crisis (2008) 31, 33
Eggins, Suzanne 14–15
emplotment 33, *34*
ethos 26, 55n2, 76
events 12, 21, 29–32
event structure analysis (ESA) 31–2
exploratory approach 65–6
extra-textual narration 48–9, *53*

fabula 21–2, 36
FC Barcelona football club 50
Fischer, Frank 10–11
flashback 38
flashforward 38
focalization *see* point of view
forgetting 3

Forster, E. M. 13
fractal analogue 60–2, *61*, *66*
France 26–7
frequency 44, *45*
future 4–5, *35*, 35–6

Gamper, Joan 50
Geertz, Clifford 81
Genette, Gérard 12
George VI (King of Great Britain) 4, 9–10, 20, 22, *35*, 35–7, 45–6, 54, 56, 66–8, 81
Goldstein, Kenneth 23, 78
Global Language Monitor 10
Goffman, Erving 49

Heise, David R. 32
Herman, David 6, 19, 21
histoire vs. discours 22
historical approach 65
historiography 70

identity, narrative 3–4, 11
implication 31
implied readers/audiences 52–3
implied speakers/authors 51–2, *53*
intertextuality 74

Jefferson, Thomas 26
Johnson, Lyndon 30–1

kernels 32, *34*
King, Martin Luther, Jr. 43
Kristeva, Julia 74

Labov, William 12, 14
Levi Strauss & Co. 41
Linde, Charlotte 23

MacKinnon, Catharine 57
Mandelbrot, Benoît 60
Mandelbrot sets 60–1, *61*
March for Jobs and Freedom 43
master narratives 25, *34*
meaningfulness 13–14
MidWest Insurance Company 23
Mink, Louis 13–14, 71
Mishler, Elliott G. 71
mobility, narrative 77
multiplicity: about 56; defined *19*, *66*; demonstrating study of 66–8; fractal analogue 60–2, *61*; historical approach 65; imagining 65–6; importance of 18; new means for 59; normative perspective in 77–9; oriented 84–6, *85*; power of 57–9; in social narratives 57–9; structural approach 62–5, *63*; study of 59–68
multi-text stories 24–5

narration: about 47; defined 16, *19*, 47, *53*; demonstrating study of 54; extra-textual 48–9, *53*; implied authors/speakers/audiences 51–3; normative perspective in 74–7; study of 47–54; textual 49–51, *53*
"Narrative and Chaos" (Argyros) 60
narrative identity 3–4, 11
narrative mobility 77
narrative research in the social sciences 10–11
narratives: collective 17; concise 62–5, *63*, *66*; defining 11–17, 70–1; importance of 2; master 25, *34*; minimalist definition of 15–16; persuasive effects of 2–3; social, defined 17–18, *19*; studying large number of 85–6; Zionist 64–5; *see also specific topics*
narrative triplet 16–17; *see also* narration; stories; text
narratology 5–6, 8nn1–2, 18, 21, 22, 25, 38, 50
national stories 23, 25, 26–7, 50
non-character narrators 50–1, *53*
normative perspective: about 69; dilemmas in study of social narratives 79; in multiplicity 77–9; in narration 74–7; in story 69–73; in text 73–4

Obama, Barack 31, 33
Ochs, Elinor 2
order 43, 44, *45*
oriented multiplicity 84–6, *85*

Palin, Sarah 57–8
Parks, Rosa 75
peacemaking stories 33–4
persuasive effects of narratives 2–3
Plato 9
plot, as term 32
plot types 32–4, *34*
point of view 39–41, *45*
political discourse 13, 35
political stories 4–5, 30–1, 33–4
Polkinghorne 11–12, 41, 87n1
prerequisite relations 31
principals 49, *53*
proximity between stories 78–9

readers, implied 52–3
reality 69–73
reconstructing stories 27, *28*, 29, *34*, 36, 83
re-mediation 57
Ricoeur, Paul 11, 70
Rimmon-Kenan, Shlomith 15, 16–17, 42, 43–4

satellites *see* catalysts
Scott, James C. 74
Sheafer, Tamir 23, 27, 78
Shifman, Limor 58–9
Simpson, O. J. 72
sjuzhet 22, 36
Slade, Diana 14–15
social cognition 78
social domain: characters in 25–7; stories in 22–4; *see also specific topics*
social narratives, defined 17–18, *19*; *see also specific topics*
social narratology 8
social reality 69–73
social sciences, narrative research in 10–11
Some Like It Hot (film) 21
South Africa (constitution) 50
Sparks, Holloway 75
speakers 51–2, *53*, 76
stories: about 27, *28*, 29; competing 78; concept of 20–1; defined 16, *19*, *34*; demonstrating study of *35*, 35–6; dominant 75, 77–8; events, relations between 29–32; multi-text 24–5; national 23, 25, 26–7, 50; normative perspective in 69–73; peacemaking 33–4; plot and plot types 32–4; political 4–5, 30–1, 33–4; proximity between 78–9; reality and 69–73;

reconstructing 27, *28*, 29, *34*, 36, 83; in social domain 22–4; study of 27–36; tellability of 75; telling, reasons for 2–3; text and 24–5, 38–9; text *versus* 21–2; *see also specific topics*
story-lines 6, 24
story-time 41, 42–3, *45*
storyworld 21, *34*
structural approach 14–15, 62–5, *63*
Superman 21

Tannen, Deborah 25
Tea Party movement 57–8
technologies, new 59
tellability of stories 75
text: about 37; coding 27, *28*; defined 16, *19*, 37, *45*; demonstrating study of 45–6; necessity of 37–9; normative perspective in 73–4; order, duration, and frequency 43–4; point of view 39–41; story and 24–5, 38–9; story *versus* 21–2; study of 39–46; time, text, and context 41–3
text-time 41–2, *45*
textual narration 49–51, *53*
King's Speech, The (film) 9, 67
themes 27
thin and thick perspectives 81–4, *82*, 86
time-theme 60, 62–5, *63*, *66*
transportation theory 2–3

Vietnam War 30–1
Vinitzky-Seroussi, Vered 27

"We Are the 99 Percent" meme 58–9
White, Hayden 14, 33, 70–1
World Health Organization (WHO) 32